FUN WITH CHINESE CHARACTERS

The Straits Times Collection ②

Cartoonist: Tan Huay Peng

FEDERAL PUBLICATIONS

An imprint of Times Media

Published in 1982 for The Straits Times
by Federal Publications (S) Pte Ltd
An imprint of Times Media Private Limited
A member of the Times Publishing Group
Times Centre
1 New Industrial Road
Singapore 536196
Tel: (65) 284 8844 Fax: (65) 285 4871
Email: te@tpl.com.sg

Online Bookstore:
http://www.timesone.com.sg/te

Times Subang
Lot 46, Subang Hi-Tech Industrial Park
Batu Tiga
40000 Shah Alam
Selangor Darul Ehsan
Malaysia
Tel & Fax: (603) 5636 3517
Email: cchong@tpg.com.my

Reprinted 1982, 1983 (twice), 1985 (twice), 1986, 1987 (twice),
1988 (twice), 1989, 1990, 1991 (twice), 1992 (twice), 1993,
1994 (twice), 1999, 2000, 2001

ISBN 981 013 005 8

Printed by Press Ace Pte Ltd

PREFACE

This book is for those who enjoy the imaginative and humorous interpretations of Chinese characters seen through the discerning eye of a cartoonist. It is the sequel to *Fun with Chinese Characters Volume 1* which has met with gratifying success.

As in Volume 1, the 153 cartoons first appeared as a regular feature in *The Straits Times* Bilingual Page. They introduce systematically the radical elements and their compounds, together with related or associated characters.

Have more fun, then, with Chinese characters!

CONTENTS 目录

105	龟	guī	118	受	shòu	131	风	fēng
106	万	wàn	119	骨	gǔ	132	公	gōng
107	易	yì	120	皮	pí	133	私	sī
108	龙	lóng	121	假	jiǎ	134	丝	sī
109	角	jiǎo	122	须	xū	135	线	xiàn
110	解	jiě	123	头	tóu	136	红	hóng
111	毛	máo	124	虫	chóng	137	给	geǐ
112	尾	wěi	125	蚁	yǐ	138	结	jié
113	老	lǎo	126	蜂	fēng	139	纸	zhǐ
114	票	piào	127	蝶	dié	140	网	wǎng
115	爬	pá	128	虾	xiā	141	细	xì
116	为	wèi or wéi	129	蛇	shé	142	经	jīng
117	争	zhēng	130	蛋	dàn	143	终	zhōng

144	维	wéi
145	罗	luó
146	乐	yuè or lè
147	药	yào
148	学	xué
149	写	xiě
150	印	yìn
151	书	shū
152	画	huà
153	事	shì

聪 (聰)

CŌNG   intelligent; clever

THIS character enlarges on 悤 (excitement, haste) by adding the ear radical (耳) to produce 聰, suggesting quickness at hearing or grasping ideas, i.e., intelligent. The simplified form ingeniously combines 耳 (ear) with 总 (general, comprehensive) to convey the idea of cleverness at hearing and comprehending things generally: 聪.

一 丆 丁 𠃋 耳 耳 耴 耴 耴 耴 耴 聪 聪 聪

聪慧	cōng huì	bright; intelligent
聪明	cōng míng	intelligent
聪颖	cōng yǐng	bright; clever

Example

他 很 聪 明 。

Tā hěn cōng míng

He is very intelligent.

HUÌ

wit;
wisdom

TWO leafy branches (艹) held in the hand (彐) improvise a broom (彗). Broom (彗) placed over heart (心) clears the way for wit and wisdom. Hence: 慧 — a heart swept clean, ready to receive the proverbial counsel: "Man combs his hair every morning; why not his heart?"

慧心	huì xīn	wisdom
慧眼	huì yǎn	mental discernment
智慧	zhì huì	wisdom

Example

你 的 话 充 满 智 慧 。
Nǐ · de huà chōng mǎn zhì huì
Your words are full of wisdom.

2

È or Wù   evil

IN the phonetic: 亞 (ugly), the vertical line is doubled to indicate imperfection and deformity. The two horizontal lines (二) signify second or inferior. Pictographically, 亞 suggests two hunchbacks facing each other, representing ugliness. 亞 (ugliness) collaborates with the heart (心) to breed evil: 惡, stirring up in the mind the proverbial exhortation: "See no evil; hear no evil; speak no evil; and do no evil."

一	丁	丌	兀	西	亚	亚	恶	恶	恶		

恶毒	è dú	malicious		恶心	è xīn	nauseating
恶化	è huà	worsen		恶意	è yì	ill-will
恶劣	è liè	harsh; abominable		可恶	kě wù	hateful
恶习	è xí	bad habits				

Example

他 很 可 恶 。
Tā hěn kě wù.

He is very hateful.

3

ĒN

恩

mercy;
kindness;
grace

WHY is a mature man (大) confined in a cell or enclosure (囗)? The answer forms the character: 因, meaning cause or reason. The sight of such a confined man may excite pity in the heart (心), and if this feeling leads one to liberate him, that is grace or mercy — the result of tempering reason (因) with sentiment (心).

丨 冂 月 冈 冈 因 因 恩 恩 恩

恩爱	ēn ài	conjugal love; loving	恩人	ēn rén	benefactor
恩赐	ēn cì	bestow (favours, charity, etc)	恩怨	ēn yuàn	resentment; grievance
恩德	ēn dé	kindness; grace	恩泽	ēn zé	bounties bestowed by a monarch or an official
恩典	ēn diǎn	favour; grace			
恩惠	ēn huì	favour; kindness	恩将仇报	ēn jiāng chóu bào	requite kindness with enmity
恩情	ēn qíng	loving-kindness			

Example

他 们 是 一 对 恩 爱 的 夫 妻 。

Tā‧men shì yí duì ēn ài‧de fū qī.

They are an affectionate couple.

4

HÉ

unite; join

THE upper portion of this character is made up of three lines joined together to form a balanced triangle: △, indicating "together". The lower part is the character for "mouth": 口 . Hence: 合 – three mouths (口) together (△), i.e., unity and understanding — a very rare occurrence, as the saying goes: "If three persons can agree entirely, then the earth can be changed to gold."

丿 人 △ 合 合 合

合唱	hé chàng	chorus	
合法	hé fǎ	legal; lawful	
合格	hé gé	qualified; up to standard	
合伙	hé huǒ	form a partnership	
合计	hé jì	add up to; amount to; total	

合理	hé lǐ	reasonable; rational
合身	hé shēn	fit
合同	hé tóng	contract
合意	hé yì	be to one's liking
合作	hé zuò	cooperate; work together

Example

他 是 一 个 合 格 的 记 者 。

Tā shì yī gè hé gé·de jì zhě.

He is a qualified reporter.

 **(僉)**

QIĀN   unanimous; all together

僉 is a coming together (亼) of mouths (口口) and persons (从). 亼 signifies together; 口口 indicates the clamour of voices; and 从 represents persons, one following another. 僉 therefore means unanimous or all together. Coincidentally, 僉 bears a striking resemblance to the face in a crowd and, clarified by the flesh radical (月), stands for face:臉.

ノ	人	亼	仐	佥	命	金							

佥谋	qiān móu	plan decided by all
佥议	qiān yì	public opinion

Example

这 是 一 项 佥 谋
Zhè shì yí xiàng qiān móu.

This is a plan decided by all.

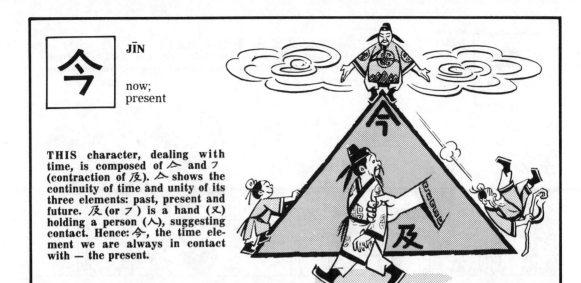

今 JĪN

now; present

THIS character, dealing with time, is composed of 亼 and ㇆ (contraction of 及). 亼 shows the continuity of time and unity of its three elements: past, present and future. 及 (or ㇆) is a hand (又) holding a person (人), suggesting contact. Hence: 今, the time element we are always in contact with — the present.

ノ	人	亼	今									

今后	jīn hòu	from now on
今年	jīn nián	this year
今天	jīn tiān	today
今生	jīn shēng	this life
今昔	jīn xī	the present and the past
今译	jīn yì	modern translation

Example

今　天　的　天　气　真　好　。
Jīn tiān·de tiān qì zhēn hǎo.

The weather today is very good.

7

念 **NIÀN**

read; recite

THE components of 念 are 今 (present) and 心 (heart). 念 is to bring to mind the past — by means of reading, reciting or chanting. Derived meanings include thinking, studying, remembering and even wishing to revive the past.

ノ 人 人 今 今 念 念 念

念经	niàn jīng	recite or chant scriptures
念头	niàn tóu	thought
念珠	niàn zhū	beads; rosary
观念	guān niàn	sense; idea; concept
怀念	huái niàn	cherish
纪念	jì niàn	in memory
想念	xiǎng niàn	miss (someone or something)
念念不忘	niàn niàn bù wàng	bear in mind constantly

Example

在 外 国 求 学 时 ， 我 很 想 念 妈 妈 。
Zài wài gúo qiú xué shí, wǒ hěn xiǎng niàn mā·ma.

I missed my mother very much while I was studying abroad.

8

TĀN   covet; greedy

THE presence (今) of anything precious (貝, cowrie money) arouses the emotion of covetousness or greed. Hence: 貪, to covet. Such greed enables a person to gain the things money can buy and lose the things money cannot buy.

| ノ | 人 | 스 | 今 | 今 | 含 | 贪 | 贪 | | | | | |

贪婪	tān lán	avaricious; greedy
贪图	tān tú	covet
贪污	tān wū	corruption
贪心	tān xīn	greedy
贪赃	tān zāng	take bribes; practise graft
贪便宜	tān pián·yi	keep on gaining petty advantages
贪生怕死	tān shēng pà sǐ	be mortally afraid of death
贪污调查局	tān wū diào chá jú	Corrupt Practices Investigation Board (CPIB)

Example

他 在 法 庭 被 控 贪 污 。
Tā zài fǎ tíng bèi kòng tān wū.

He is charged in court for corruption.

9

金 JĪN

gold; metal

THE original seal form: 金 showed the presence (今) of four gold nuggets (𡙻) hidden in the earth (土). The regular form reveals only two nuggets: 金. In the simplified radical form, even these two remaining nuggets are missing: 钅. However, the proverb reassures us: "True gold fears no fire." Only thieves!

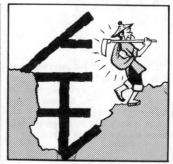

丿 人 个 今 全 全 余 金 金

金融　　　jīn róng　　　　finance
金色　　　jīn sè　　　　　golden
金鱼　　　jīn yú　　　　　goldfish
白金　　　bái jīn　　　　platinum
黄金　　　huáng jīn　　　gold
金字塔　　jīn zì tǎ　　　　pyramid
金缕玉衣　jīn lǚ yù yī　　　jade clothes sewn with gold thread
金碧辉煌　jīn bì huī huáng　grand and magnificent

Example

他 喜 欢 穿 金 色 的 衣 服 。
Tā xǐ huān chuān jīn sè .de yī fú.

He likes to wear clothes of a golden colour.

银 (銀)

YÍN   silver

SILVER is produced by consolidating 金 (gold) with 艮 (hard): 银. 艮, originally the eye (目) turned suddenly around (匕) to look a man full in the face defiantly, means "obstinate". Compared with gold, silver is a hard (艮) metal (金), more precious than common copper. Hence the saying: "Even he who has accumulated 10,000 taels of silver cannot take with him at death half a copper."

| ノ | ト | ヒ | 乍 | 金 | 钅 | 钅 | 钅 | 钅 | 银 | 银 | | | |

银杯	yín bēi	silver cup; trophy
银币	yín bì	silver coin
银行	yín háng	bank
银河	yín hé	the Milky Way (sky)
银婚	yín hūn	silver wedding
银幕	yín mù	(motion-picture) screen
银牌	yín pái	silver medal
银色	yín sè	silvery
水银	shuǐ yín	mercury

Example

他 在 一 间 银 行 工 作 。
Tā zài yī jiān yín háng gōng zuò.

He works in a bank.

11

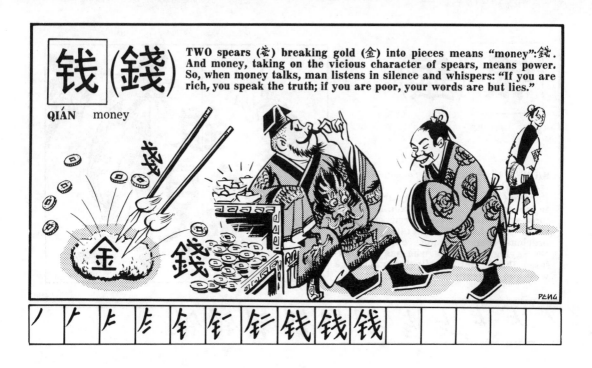

钱(錢)

QIÁN money

TWO spears (戋) breaking gold (金) into pieces means "money": 錢. And money, taking on the vicious character of spears, means power. So, when money talks, man listens in silence and whispers: "If you are rich, you speak the truth; if you are poor, your words are but lies."

丿 亻 仁 牛 金 钅 钅 钱 钱 钱

钱币	qián bì	coin
钱包	qián bāo	wallet; purse
钱财	qián cái	wealth
钱柜	qián guì	money-locker; money-box; till
捐钱	juān qián	donate money
零钱	líng qián	small change
赚钱	zhuàn qián	earn money

Example

这 个 手 表 多 少 钱 ?
Zhè gè shǒu biǎo duō shǎo qián?

How much is this watch?

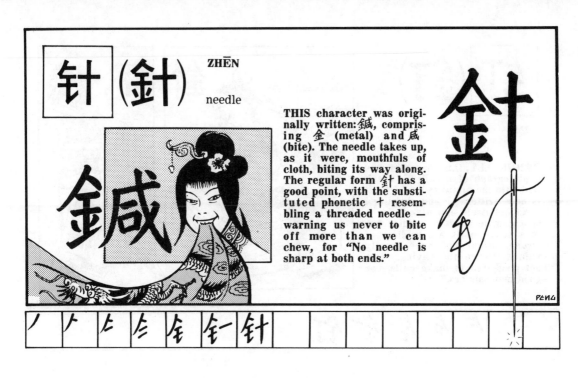

针 (針) ZHĒN

needle

THIS character was originally written: 鍼, comprising 金 (metal) and 咸 (bite). The needle takes up, as it were, mouthfuls of cloth, biting its way along. The regular form 针 has a good point, with the substituted phonetic 十 resembling a threaded needle — warning us never to bite off more than we can chew, for "No needle is sharp at both ends."

针对	zhēn duì	directed at
针灸	zhēn jiǔ	acupuncture
针线	zhēn xiàn	needlework
针眼	zhēn yǎn	the eye of a needle
针织	zhēn zhī	knitting
打针	dǎ zhēn	an injection
针刺麻醉	zhēn cì má zuì	acupuncture anaesthesia

Example

针 灸 是 中 国 人 发 明 的 。
Zhēn jiǔ shì Zhōng Guó rén fā míng·de.

Acupuncture was invented by the Chinese.

13

钉 (釘)

DĪNG　nail

ORIGINALLY, this character was a pictograph of a nail: 丁. Clarified with the metal radical (金), it is now written 釘 and simplified to 钉. 丁 itself now stands for a strong male adult or soldier for, in a sense, nails are soldiers — strong, useful but never really valued. Hence the saying: "Use not good iron to make nails, nor good men soldiers."

丿 丷 𠂉 𠂎 金 钅 钉

钉锤	dīng chuí	hammer
钉帽	dīng mào	the head of a nail
钉耙	dīng pá	(iron-toothed) rake
钉人	dīng rén	watch (or mark) an opponent in a game
钉鞋	dīng xié	spiked shoes
钉子	dīng · zi	nail
碰钉子	pèng dīng · zi	meet with a rebuff
眼中钉	yǎn zhōng dīng	thorn in one's flesh

Example

我 想 买 一 把 钉 锤 。
Wǒ xiǎng mǎi yì bǎ dīng chuí.

I wish to buy a hammer.

14

户 HÙ

door

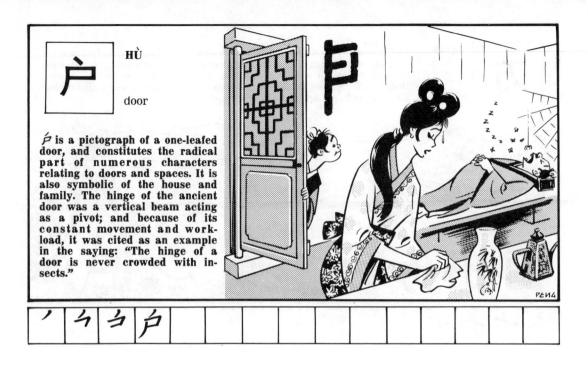

户 is a pictograph of a one-leafed door, and constitutes the radical part of numerous characters relating to doors and spaces. It is also symbolic of the house and family. The hinge of the ancient door was a vertical beam acting as a pivot; and because of its constant movement and workload, it was cited as an example in the saying: "The hinge of a door is never crowded with insects."

丶 彐 彐 户

户口	hù kǒu	household; (bank) account
户外	hù wài	outdoor
户主	hù zhǔ	head of a family
住户	zhù hù	occupants
家家户户	jiā jiā hù hù	every household

Example

他 喜 欢 户 外 活 动 。

Tā xǐ huān hù wài huó dòng.

He likes outdoor activities.

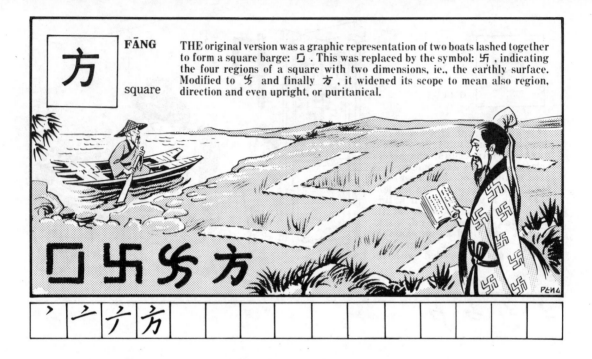

FĀNG

square

THE original version was a graphic representation of two boats lashed together to form a square barge: 口 . This was replaced by the symbol: 坊 , indicating the four regions of a square with two dimensions, ie., the earthly surface. Modified to 坊 and finally 方 , it widened its scope to mean also region, direction and even upright, or puritanical.

方便	fāng biàn	convenient
方法	fāng fǎ	method; way
方格	fāng gé	checks
方略	fāng lüè	general plan
方向	fāng xiàng	direction
方形	fāng xíng	square
方言	fāng yán	dialect
方正	fāng zhèng	upright

Example

这 张 桌 子 是 方 形 的 。

Zhè zhāng zhuō·zi shì fāng xíng·de.

This is a square table.

16

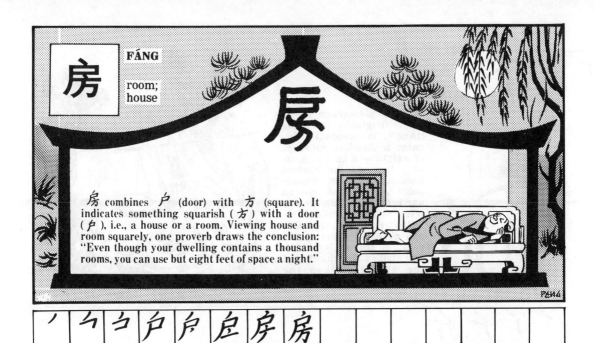

房 FÁNG

room; house

房 combines 戶 (door) with 方 (square). It indicates something squarish (方) with a door (戶), i.e., a house or a room. Viewing house and room squarely, one proverb draws the conclusion: "Even though your dwelling contains a thousand rooms, you can use but eight feet of space a night."

丿 ㇆ ㇕ 戶 戶 㡊 房 房

房舱	fáng cāng	passenger's cabin in a ship
房产	fáng chǎn	house property
房顶	fáng dǐng	roof
房基	fáng jī	foundations (of a building)
房间	fáng jiān	room

房客	fáng kè	tenant; lodger
房契	fáng qì	title deed
房屋	fáng wū	houses; buildings
房主	fáng zhǔ	house-owner
房地产	fáng dì chǎn	real estate

Example

他 将 房 产 抵 押 给 银 行 。

Tā jiāng fáng chǎn dǐ yā gěi yín háng.

He mortgaged his house to a bank.

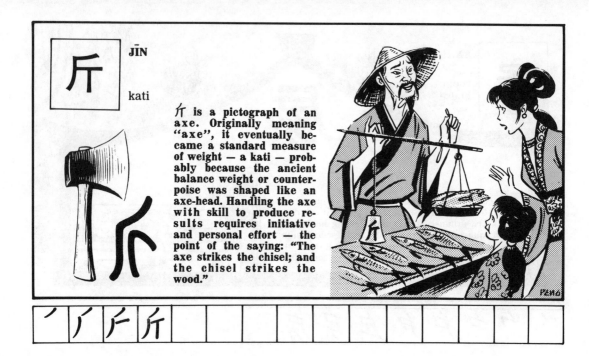

JĪN

斤

kati

斤 is a pictograph of an axe. Originally meaning "axe", it eventually became a standard measure of weight — a kati — probably because the ancient balance weight or counterpoise was shaped like an axe-head. Handling the axe with skill to produce results requires initiative and personal effort — the point of the saying: "The axe strikes the chisel; and the chisel strikes the wood."

斤两	jīn liǎng	weight
斤斤计较	jīn jīn jì jiào	be calculating
半斤八两	bàn jīn bā liǎng	not much to choose between the two

Example

这 块 石 头 重 一 斤 。
Zhè kuài shí tóu zhòng yī jīn.

This stone weighs one kati.

所 SUǑ

place

所 is a juxtaposition of 户 (door) and 斤 (axe), and refers to the place where fuel is prepared. In olden times, the chopping of firewood with the axe (斤) was done near the door or house (户). Hence: 所 (axe beside house) meaning place or location.

| ノ | ㇉ | 彐 | 户 | 户' | 所 | 所 | 所 | | | | | | |

所部	suǒ bù	troops under one's command
所得	suǒ dé	income; earnings
所谓	suǒ wèi	what is called; so-called
所以	suǒ yǐ	so; therefore; as a result
所有	suǒ yǒu	own; possess
所在	suǒ zài	place; location
所致	suǒ zhì	be the result of
所以然	suǒ yǐ rán	the reason why
所向无前	suǒ xiàng wú qián	be invincible

Example

他 所 得 的 薪 金 有 限 。
Tā suǒ dé · de xīn jīn yǒu xiàn.
He earns a small salary.

JIÀNG

artisan;
craftsman

AN artisan: 匠 is represented by his tool: 斤 (an axe) and his work: 匚 (a hollowed-out log, vessel or box). The craftsman's dependence upon his tools prompts the saying: "The workman who would do his work well should first sharpen his tools."

| 一 | 一 | 匚 | 匚 | 匠 | 匠 | | | | | | |

| | | | | | | | | | | | |

匠人	jiàng rén	artisan; craftsman
匠心	jiàng xīn	ingenuity; craftsmanship
木匠	mù jiàng	carpenter
石匠	shí jiàng	stonemason
铁匠	tiě jiàng	blacksmith

Example

他 的 作 品 独 具 匠 心 。
Tā · de zuò pǐng dú jù jiàng xīn.

His works show ingenuity.

20

BĪNG

soldier;
army

兵 is represented by two hands
(⺍ or 廾) brandishing a battle-
axe (斤) — symbol of the soldier.
Lamenting the necessity of main-
taining an army in a belligerent
world, one proverb concludes:
"Feed soldiers for a thousand days,
to be used for one day."

丿 丿 仁 斤 斤 斤 兵

兵变	bīng biàn		mutiny
兵器	bīng qì		arms
兵役	bīng yì		military service
兵营	bīng yíng		barracks
步兵	bù bīng		infantry
工兵	gōng bīng		engineer (soldier)
士兵	shì bīng		soldier
兵荒马乱	bīng huāng mǎ luàn		turmoil and chaos of war

Example

他 是 一 个 勇 敢 的 士 兵 。

Tā shì yī gè yǒng gǎn·de shì bīng.

He is a brave soldier.

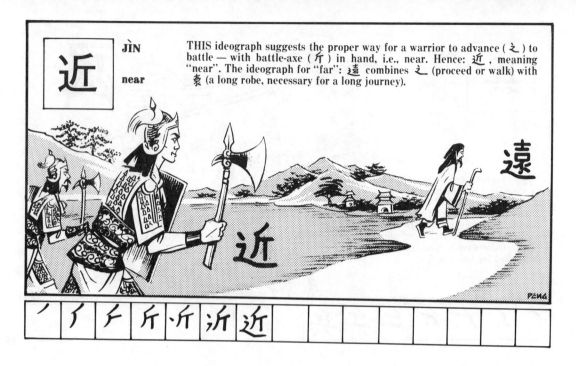

近 JÌN near

THIS ideograph suggests the proper way for a warrior to advance (之) to battle — with battle-axe (斤) in hand, i.e., near. Hence: 近 , meaning "near". The ideograph for "far": 遠 combines 之 (proceed or walk) with 袁 (a long robe, necessary for a long journey).

近海	jìn hǎi	coastal waters
近乎	jìn hū	close to
近况	jìn kuàng	recent development
近来	jìn lái	recently
近邻	jìn lín	neighbour
近亲	jìn qīn	close relatives
近视	jìn shì	myopia
附近	fù jìn	nearby

Example

我 家 附 近 有 一 间 戏 院 。
Wǒ jiā fù jìn yǒu yī jiān xì yuàn.

There is a cinema near my house.

质 (質)

ZHÌ

character; quality

TWO axes (斤), poised above a cowrie shell (貝, representing something precious), are ready to dissect it and ascertain its worth: 質. The axes ensure a complete and thorough job. Hence: 質, denoting value, quality, nature or character.

ノ	厂	厂	斤	斥	斥	质	质	

质地	zhì dì	texture
质料	zhì liào	material
质问	zhì wèn	question
质疑	zhì yí	query
本质	běn zhì	innate character
品质	pǐn zhì	quality; character
人质	rén zhì	hostage
性质	xìng zhì	nature; character

Example

这 衣 服 的 质 料 很 好 。

Zhè yī fú · de zhì liào hěn hǎo.

The material of this dress is of a high quality.

23

XĪN

new

RODS, freshly chopped from the hazel bush (亲) for flexibility, were once used for flogging criminals, sometimes to extort a confession. Hence: 新, the symbol for "new", indicated by the hazel rods (亲) and the axe (斤).

丶	二	产	立	立	辛	辛	亲	亲	新	新	新

新兵	xīn bīng	new recruit	新奇	xīn qí	strange; new; novel
新婚	xīn hūn	newly-married	新式	xīn shì	new type; latest type
新郎	xīn láng	bridegroom	新闻	xīn wén	news
新年	xīn nián	New Year	新鲜	xīn xiān	fresh
新娘	xīn niáng	bride	新大陆	xīn dà lù	the New World — the Americas

Example

这 是 一 座 新 建 的 工 厂 。

Zhè shì yī zuò xīn jiàn·de gōng chǎng.

This is a newly-built factory.

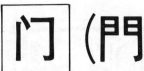

MÉN　door; gate

JUST as 戶 symbolises a one-leafed door, so 門 represents a door with two leaves. Doors provide exits and entrances, but not all are convenient, as exemplified in the proverb: "The door of charity is hard to open, and hard to shut." To simplify matters, the regular door: 門 has now been stripped down to an open doorway: 门.

ˊ	冂	门							

门齿	mén chǐ	front tooth; incisor	门牌	mén pái	house number
门第	mén dì	family status	门徒	mén tú	disciple
门户	mén hù	door	门诊	mén zhěn	outpatient service
门槛	mén kǎn	threshold	门市部	mén shì bù	sales department
门口	mén kǒu	doorway	门外汉	mén wài hàn	layman

Example

请 把 门 关 起 来 。
Qǐng bǎ mén guān qǐ · lai.

Please shut the door.

 们（們）

MÉN plural sign

THIS character has 人 (person) as radical and 門 (door) as phonetic. 門 is a door with two leaves instead of one (as in 戶). Clarified by the radical for person (人), it is the plural sign for nouns and pronouns, applied to people: 們.

| ノ | イ | イ′ | 们 | 们 | | | | | | | | | |

你们	nǐ·men	you (second person plural)
人们	rén·men	people; the public
他们	tā·men	they; them
我们	wǒ·men	we; us

Example

我 们 要 去 看 戏 。
Wǒ·men yào qù kàn xì.

We are going to see a show.

问 (問)

WÈN ask; enquire; question

ENQUIRIES are often made at the door, the entrance to a house. A mouth (口) at the door (門) therefore becomes a fitting ideograph for ask or enquire: 問. It can also mean question or interrogate, although to do so in an officious manner would be, according to the saying, "asking the blind man the way." (问道于盲)

'	亻	门	冋	问	问						

问答	wèn dá	questions and answers	问题	wèn tí	question; problem
问好	wèn hǎo	send one's regards to another person	问讯	wèn xùn	inquire; ask
问号	wèn hào	question mark	问罪	wèn zuì	denounce; condemn
问候	wèn hòu	extend greetings to someone	盘问	pán wèn	interrogate; cross-examination
问世	wèn shì	be published; come out	审问	shěn wèn	interrogate

Example

他 问 我 今 年 几 岁 。
Tā wèn wǒ jīn nián jǐ suì.

He asked for my age.

闻 (聞)

WÉN

hear; news

IN this ideograph, "ear" (耳) becomes "hear" (聞) when placed at the door (門). By extension 聞 also means "news", for the ear (耳) is the door (門) of knowledge or information. But not all news obtained by the ear is reliable, as the saying goes: "What the ear hears is not equal to what the eye sees."

闻名	wén míng	famous
闻人	wén rén	celebrity
丑闻	chǒu wén	scandal
新闻	xīn wén	news
要闻	yào wén	important news
听而不闻	tīng' ér bù wén	turn deaf ear to
闻风丧胆	wén fēng sàng dǎn	become terror-stricken at the news
闻所未闻	wén suǒ wèi wén	unheard of

Example

今 天 的 新 闻 真 多 ！
Jīn tiān · de xīn wén zhēn duō !

There is so much news today!

28

开 (開)

KĀI open

A bar or bolt (一) across the door (門) means to shut (閂). Two hands (廾) taking away the bar (一) signifies to open: 開 . But there is more to the business of opening than just unbolting the door. As the proverb says: "To open a shop is easy; the difficult thing is to keep it open."

一 二 于 开

开办	kāi bàn	set up; establish	
开采	kāi cǎi	mine; extract	
开除	kāi chú	expel	
开刀	kāi dāo	perform a surgical operation	
开动	kāi dòng	start	

开端	kāi duān	beginning
开幕	kāi mù	inaugurate; open
开始	kāi shǐ	start
开通	kāi tōng	liberal; open-minded
公开	gōng kāi	open (adj)

Example

请 你 把 门 打 开 。
Qǐng nǐ bǎ mén dǎ kāi.

Please open the door.

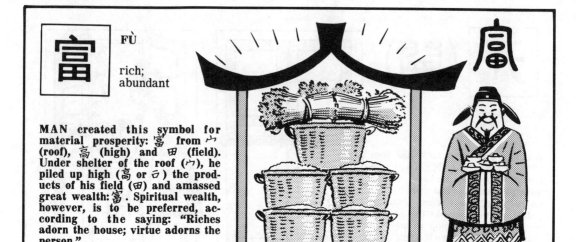

富 FÙ

rich;
abundant

MAN created this symbol for material prosperity: 富 from 宀 (roof), 高 (high) and 田 (field). Under shelter of the roof (宀), he piled up high (高 or 口) the products of his field (田) and amassed great wealth: 富. Spiritual wealth, however, is to be preferred, according to the saying: "Riches adorn the house; virtue adorns the person."

| 丶 | 八 | 宀 | 宀 | 宀 | 宀 | 富 | 富 | 富 | 富 | 富 | 富 | | | |

富丽	fù lì	grand; magnificent
富强	fù qiáng	prosperous and strong
富饶	fù ráo	bountiful; fertile
富庶	fù shù	rich and abundant
富翁	fù wēng	wealthy man
富裕	fù yù	wealthy
富国强民	fù guó qiáng mín	to enrich the country and strengthen its people
富丽堂皇	fù lì táng huáng	gorgeous; splendid

Example

他 的 家 庭 很 富 裕 。
Tā · de jiā tíng hěn fù yù.

His family is very wealthy.

30

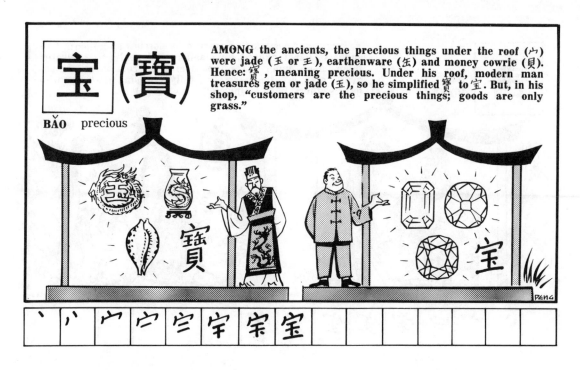

宝 (寶)

BǍO precious

AMONG the ancients, the precious things under the roof (宀) were jade (玉 or 王) and money cowrie (貝). Hence: 寶, meaning precious. Under his roof, modern man treasures gem or jade (玉), so he simplified 寶 to 宝. But, in his shop, "customers are the precious things; goods are only grass."

丶 丷 宀 宀 宀 宇 宝 宝

宝贝	bǎo bèi	treasured object; baby
宝贵	bǎo guì	valuable; precious
宝剑	bǎo jiàn	a double-edged sword
宝库	bǎo kù	treasure-house
宝石	bǎo shí	precious stone; gem
宝物	bǎo wù	treasure
宝藏	bǎo zàng	precious (mineral) deposits
宝座	bǎo zuò	throne

Example

这 颗 宝 石 值 一 万 元 。
Zhè kē bǎo shí zhí yī wàn yuán.

This gem is worth ten thousand dollars.

31

害 **HÀI**

harm;
injure

≢ represents a stick (|) marred by notches (彡); mouth (口) suggests harm caused by slander; and roof (宀) indicates injury done under cover, i.e., secretly. From these components man created harm: 害, fully realising that "he who harms others, harms himself." (害人反害己)

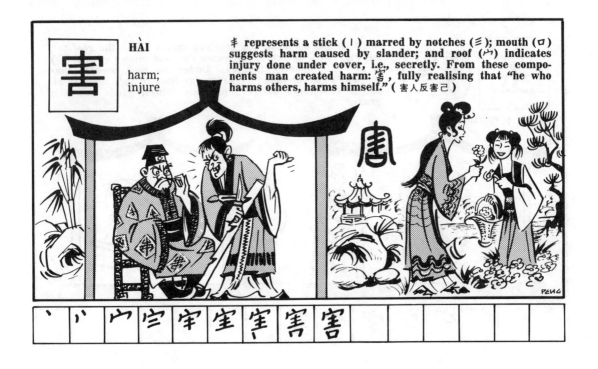

`丶 丷 宀 宁 宔 宝 害 害 害`

害虫	hài chóng	harmful insect	除害	chú hài	eliminate evil
害处	hài chù	harm	利害	lì hài	terrible; formidable
害怕	hài pà	afraid	灾害	zāi hài	calamity; disaster
害臊	hài sào	feel ashamed	害人虫	hài rén chóng	an evil creature; pest; vermin
害羞	hài xiū	bashful; shy	害群之马	hài qún zhī mǎ	one who brings disgrace to his group — black sheep

Example

老 鼠 害 人 不 浅 。
Lǎo shǔ hài rén bù qiǎn.
Mice do people great harm.

32

DÌNG

fix;
decide;
certain

THIS character is made up of roof (宀) and order (正 or 疋). It signifies peace and order under the roof, implanting the idea of fixed, certain or decided: 定. Order under the roof comes before order under the heavens, although the proverb states in no uncertain terms: "It is for man to plan, but for Heaven to decide."

`丶 丷 宀 宀 宁 宇 定 定`

定单	dìng dān	order form	
定购	dìng gòu	order	
定婚	dìng hūn	be engaged	
定价	dìng jià	fixed price	
定居	dìng jū	settle down	

定理	dìng lǐ	theorem
否定	fǒu dìng	deny; negative
决定	jué dìng	decide
肯定	kěn dìng	positive; confirm
一定	yī dìng	surely

Example

我 定 购 了 一 辆 新 车 。
Wǒ dìng gòu·le yī liàng xīn chē.

I have ordered a new car.

WÁN

finish;
complete

THIS ideograph places roof (宀) over head (元). 元 means that which is upon (上 or 二) a person (人 or 儿), i.e., the head, origin or principle. So, putting on the roof (宀) over the head (元) finishes (完) the building. Hence: 完, the end.

完备	wán bèi	complete	完满	wán mǎn	satisfactory; successful
完毕	wán bì	finish; complete	完美	wán měi	perfect, flawless
完成	wán chéng	accomplish; complete	完全	wán quán	whole; complete
完稿	wán gǎo	complete the manuscript	完善	wán shàn	perfect
完结	wán jié	end; be over; finish	完整	wán zhěng	complete; intact

Example

我 的 信 笺 用 完 了 。
Wǒ · de xìng jiān yòng wán · le.
My letter-heads have been used up.

34

刀 **DĀO** knife

THIS radical is a pictograph of a knife or sword. Wielded in the cause of justice, the sword protects the innocent; but brandished irresponsibly, it is double-edged. A sharp blade is likened to a person vested with too much power, and a proverb warns: "A knife that's too sharp easily cuts the fingers."

刀背	dāo bèi	the back of a knife blade
刀叉	dāo chā	knife and fork
刀锋	dāo fēng	the point or edge of a knife
刀架	dāo jià	tool carrier
刀具	dāo jù	cutting tool; tool

刀片	dāo piàn	razor blade
刀枪	dāo qiāng	sword and spear; weapons
刀鞘	dāo qiào	sheath; scabbard
刀子	dāo · zi	small knife; pocketknife
刀俎	dāo zǔ	butcher's knife and chopping block

Example

我 们 用 刀 叉 来 吃 牛 扒 。

Wǒ · men yòng dāo chā lái chī niú pá.

We ate the steak with knife and fork.

35

FĒN

divide;
separate

THIS ideograph is made up
of 八 (divide), and clarified
by radical 刀 (knife) to en-
force the idea of dividing or
separating: 八. It is like
dividing (八) with a knife
(刀). 分 is used also for any
small division, component or
part, e.g., a minute, a mark
or a cent.

ノ	八	公	分											

分别	fēn bié	differentiate	分类	fēn lèi	classify
分布	fēn bù	be distributed	分裂	fēn liè	split; break up
分担	fēn dān	share responsibility	分配	fēn pèi	distribute; allot
分界	fēn jiè	boundary	分期	fēn qī	by stages
分居	fēn jū	live apart	分析	fēn xī	analyse
分开	fēn kāi	separate; part	分类广告	fēn lèi guǎng gào	classified advertisements

Example

我 要 登 一 则 分 类 广 告 。
Wǒ yào dēng yì zé fēn lèi guǎng gào.

I want to place a classified advertisement.

LÌ

benefit; gain

禾

刀

APPLYING the sickle: 刂 (a variant of 刀) to the grain (禾) suggests reaping the harvest, i.e., profit, benefit or interest: 利 . Often two parties quarrel, and a third party reaps the harvest. When the oyster and the heron fight, the saying goes: "The fisherman benefits." (鹬蚌相争，渔人得利 .)

利

PENG

'	⺌	千	矛	禾	利	利						

利弊	lì bì	pros and cons
利害	lì hài	terrible; formidable
利率	lì lǜ	rate of interest
利润	lì rùn	profit
利息	lì xī	interest
利益	lì yì	interest: benefits
利用	lì yòng	utilise; make use of
利爪	lì zhǎo	sharp claws

Example

这 家 银 行 的 利 率 很 高 。
Zhè jiā yín háng·de lì lǜ hěn gāo.

The interest rate of this bank is very high.

37

别 BIÉ

separate; depart

THE primitive form of this character combined 咼 (pictograph of a bone) with 刂 (knife). 咼 was conventionalised to 另 and then 另. The completed character: 别 signifies the knife (刂) separating flesh from bone (另) and stands for separate, depart or differ.

| 丶 | 冖 | 口 | 尸 | 另 | 别 | 别 | | | | | |

别号	bié hào	alias	别针	bié zhēn	safety pin; pin; brooch
别离	bié lí	leave	别致	bié zhì	unique
别名	bié míng	another name	别字	bié zì	wrongly written words
别人	bié rén	other people	别出心裁	bié chū xīn cái	try to be different
别墅	bié shù	villa	别具一格	bié jù yī gé	having a unique style

Example

他 常 常 写 别 字 。

Tā cháng cháng xiě bié zì.

He always writes the wrong words.

GŌNG

bow

弓 is a radical representing a Chinese bow: ฿. The ancient form shows it bent or vibrating: |ℰ. Drawing the string (|) of the bow (弓) produces the character 引, meaning to pull, guide or introduce. Though the bow is a lethal weapon for offence and defence, the proverb counsels: "Draw your bow, but don't shoot."

弓箭	gōng jiàn	bow and arrow
弓弦	gōng xián	bowstring
弓形	gōng xíng	arch-shaped

Example

这 把 弓 被 他 折 断 了 。
Zhè bǎ gōng bèi tā zhé duàn · le.

This bow was broken by him.

39

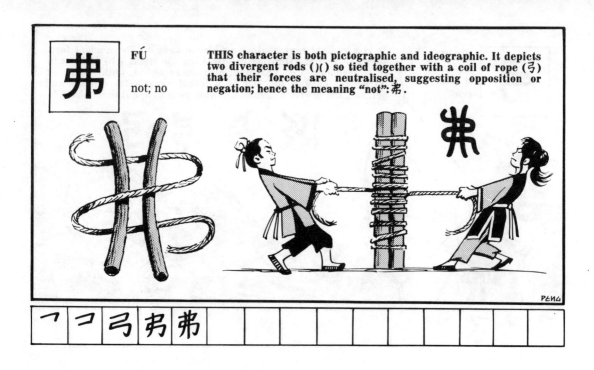

弗 FÚ

not; no

THIS character is both pictographic and ideographic. It depicts two divergent rods ( )( ) so tied together with a coil of rope (弓) that their forces are neutralised, suggesting opposition or negation; hence the meaning "not": 弗 .

自愧弗如　*zì kuèi fú rú*　feel ashamed of one's inferiority

Example

他 只 读 到 小 学 三 年 级 ， 因 此 常 常 自 愧 弗 如 。
Tā zhǐ dú dào xiǎo xué sān nián jí, yīn cí cháng cháng zì kuèi fú rú.

He had only three years of primary education, so he often has a sense of inferiority.

40

费（費）

FÈI expenses; squander

THE phonetic: 弗, representing two rods bent in opposite directions being bound together, means "not". 貝 is a picture of a cowrie shell, once used as money. 弗 placed over 貝 therefore signifies under-valuing money, by inference, to waste or squander: 費.

费解	fèi jiě	obscure; hard to understand
费力	fèi lì	strenuous
费时	fèi shí	time-consuming
费用	fèi yòng	expenses
会费	huì fèi	membership dues

浪费	làng fèi	waste; squander
免费	miǎn fèi	free of charge
学费	xué fèi	school fees
生活费	shēng huó fèi	living expenses
水电费	shuǐ diàn fèi	charges for water and electricity

Example

今 天 我 们 要 交 学 费 。

Jīn tiān wǒ ·men yào jiāo xué fèi.

We must pay school fees today.

41

剃 TÌ
shave

剃 combines 弟 (younger brother) with 刂 (knife or razor). 弟, the phonetic, depicts a thread round a spindle and means, by extension, a succession of brothers or younger brothers. The growing hair is suggested by the thread being unwound from the spindle (弟), and the addition of the razor (刂) gives us the character for shave: 剃. Our picture, however, shows how younger brother (弟) and razor (刂), put together, can mean a close shave.

丶	ﾝ	ﾝﾞ	ﾝﾞ	弜	弟	弟	剃	剃					

剃刀	tì dāo	razor
剃度	tì dù	tonsure
剃头	tì tóu	haircutting

Example

他 用 剃 刀 剃 头 。

Tā yòng tì dāo tì tóu.

He uses the razor to shave his head.

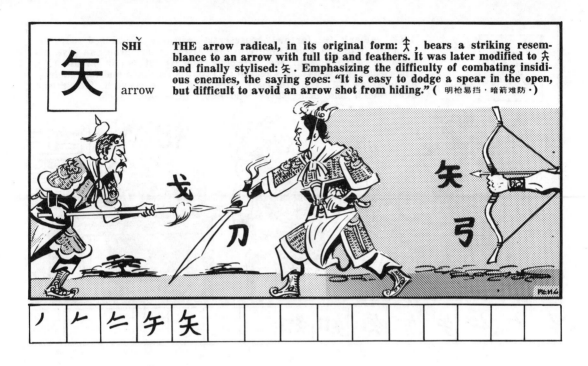

SHǏ

矢

arrow

THE arrow radical, in its original form: 夫, bears a striking resemblance to an arrow with full tip and feathers. It was later modified to 夫 and finally stylised: 矢. Emphasizing the difficulty of combating insidious enemies, the saying goes: "It is easy to dodge a spear in the open, but difficult to avoid an arrow shot from hiding." (明枪易挡，暗箭难防 ·)

| ノ | ̀ | ̀ | 午 | 矢 | | | | | | | | |

矢量	shǐ liàng	vector
飞矢	fēi shǐ	flying arrow
风矢	fēng shǐ	wind vector
矢口否认	shǐ kǒu fǒu rèn	flatly deny
无的放矢	wú dì fàng shǐ	shoot at random – not to the point

Example

他 的 批 评 有 如 无 的 放 矢 。
Tā · de pī píng yǒu rú wú dì fàng shǐ.

His criticism is like random shooting.

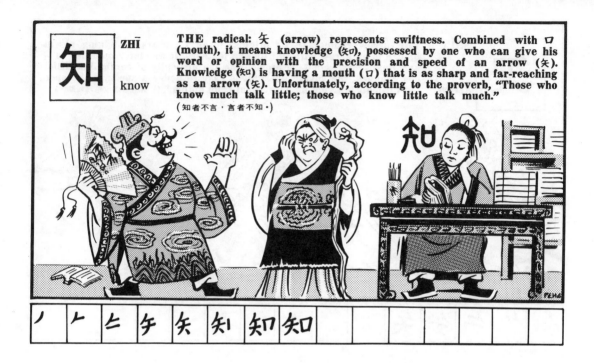

知 **ZHĪ**
know

THE radical: 矢 (arrow) represents swiftness. Combined with 口 (mouth), it means knowledge (知), possessed by one who can give his word or opinion with the precision and speed of an arrow (矢). Knowledge (知) is having a mouth (口) that is as sharp and far-reaching as an arrow (矢). Unfortunately, according to the proverb, "Those who know much talk little; those who know little talk much."

（知者不言，言者不知．）

丿 亠 二 午 矢 知 知 知

知道	zhī dào	know
知底	zhī dǐ	know the inside story
知己	zhī jǐ	bosom friend
知交	zhī jiāo	bosom friend
知觉	zhī jué	consciousness
知名	zhī míng	well-known
知识	zhī‧shi	knowledge

知难而退	zhī nán ér tuì	shrink back from difficulties
知情达理	zhī qíng dá lǐ	sensible
（或	(or	
通情达理）	tōng qíng dā lǐ)	
知识分子	zhī‧shi fèn zǐ	an intellectual

Example

我 不 知 道 她 已 经 结 婚 了 。
Wǒ bù zhī dào tā yǐ jīng jié hūn‧le.

I didn't know that she is married.

44

酒 JIǓ

liquor; wine; spirit

酉 is a pictograph of an amphora used for distilling. The radical for liquid (氵) added to it indicates the jar is filled with liquor: 酒 — wine as exhilarating and stimulating as knowledge. But liquor is intoxicating, so the proverb cautions: "Wine should be taken in small doses; knowledge in large."

丶 冫 氵 氵 汀 沔 洒 洒 洒 酒

酒吧	jiǔ bā	bar
酒菜	jiǔ cài	food and liquor
酒店	jiǔ diàn	hotel; wineshop
酒会	jiǔ huì	banquet
酒家	jiǔ jiā	restaurant
酒窖	jiǔ jiào	wine cellar

酒精	jiǔ jīng	alcohol; ethyl alcohol
酒量	jiǔ liàng	capacity for liquor
酒徒	jiǔ tú	wine bibber
酒窝	jiǔ wō	dimple
酒意	jiǔ yì	tipsy
酒肉朋友	jiǔ ròu péng yǒu	fair-weather friends

Example

他 常 常 去 酒 吧 。

Tā cháng cháng qù jiǔ bā.

He goes to the bars very often.

45

ZUÌ

醉

drunk

THIS ideograph combines the container for liquor: 酉 with the phonetic: 卒, representing a soldier. As soldiers do not last long, 卒 also means: "to come to an end." So, to drink liquor (酉) and reach the limit (卒), is to become drunk: 醉. But, suggests the proverb, "If you want a way to stop drinking, look at a drunken man when you are sober."

| 一 | 丆 | 丌 | 丙 | 西 | 西 | 酉 | 酉 | 酉 | 酉 | 酉 | 酉 | 酉 | 醉 |

醉鬼	zuì guǐ	drunkard
醉汉	zuì hàn	drunkard
醉态	zuì tài	the state of being drunk; drunkenness
醉心	zuì xīn	be bent on; engrossed in
醉眼	zuì yǎn	eyes showing the effects of drink
醉意	zuì yì	signs or feeling of becoming drunk
醉醺醺	zuì xūn xūn	drunk; tipsy
醉生梦死	zuì shēng mèng sǐ	lead a befuddled life

Example

他 喝 醉 了 。

Tā hē zuì · le.

He is drunk.

46

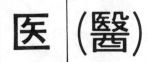

YĪ   cure; heal

ANCIENT man attributed sickness to evil influences. Healing: 醫 , therefore, was symbolised by drawing arrows from the quiver (医) to shoot (殳) at the demon of disease. Wine (酉) was indispensable as an elixir. Although the modern form of healing is very much simplified: 医 , the saying still goes: "A wise doctor never treats himself."

一 丆 丆 匸 亐 矢 医

医科	yī kē	medicine (a subject)
医疗	yī liáo	medical treatment
医生；医师	yī shēng；yī shī	doctor
医术	yī shù	medical skill
医药	yī yào	medicine
医院	yī yuàn	hospital
医治	yī zhì	cure; treat

军医	jūn yī	medical officer (in the army)
牙医	yá yī	dental surgeon
外科医生	wài kē yī shēng	surgeon
专科医生	zhuān kē yī shēng	specialist doctor
新加坡 中央医院	Xīn Jiā Pō Zhōng Yāng Yī Yuàn	Singapore General Hospital

Example

这 位 医 生 很 出 名 。
Zhè wèi yī shēng hěn chū míng.

This doctor is very famous.

47

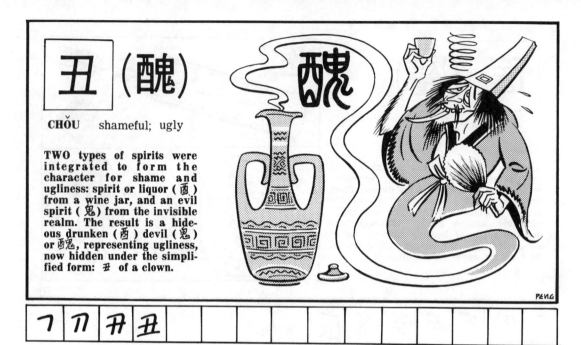

丑 (醜)

CHǑU shameful; ugly

TWO types of spirits were integrated to form the character for shame and ugliness: spirit or liquor (酉) from a wine jar, and an evil spirit (鬼) from the invisible realm. The result is a hideous drunken (酉) devil (鬼) or 酉鬼, representing ugliness, now hidden under the simplified form: 丑 of a clown.

			丑								
フ	ㄱ刀	丑	丑								

丑恶	chǒu'è	ugly; repulsive
丑化	chǒu huà	smear; defame
丑角	chǒu jué	clown
丑陋	chǒu lòu	ugly
丑事；丑闻	chǒu shì; chǒu wén	scandal
丑态	chǒu tài	ugly performance
出丑	chū chǒu	make a fool of oneself
小丑	xiǎo chǒu	clown
丑八怪	chǒu bā guài	a very ugly person

Example

家 丑 不 可 外 扬 。
Jiā chǒu bù kě wài yáng.

Don't wash your dirty linen in public.

48

GǑU

狗

dog

THIS character for dog: 狗 fittingly combines the dog radical: 犭 (or 犬) with the phonetic: 句 . 句 , meaning a sentence of words, suggests barking — a distinguishing characteristic of the dog. Counselling against the thoughtless ill-treatment of the underdog, the proverb warns: "In beating a dog, first find out who the owner is."

丿 犭 犭 犭 狗 狗 狗 狗

狗熊	gǒu xióng	black bear
海狗	hǎi gǒu	fur seal; ursine seal
狗腿子	gǒu tuǐ·zi	hired thug; lackey; henchman
狗胆包天	gǒu dǎn bāo tiān	monstrous audacity
狗眼看人低	gǒu yǎn kàn rén dī	snobbish
狗咬吕洞宾	gǒu yǎo Lǚ Dòng Bīn	mistake a good man for a bad one

Example

我 家 有 一 条 小 狗 。
Wǒ jiā yǒu yī tiáo xiǎo gǒu.

I have a puppy at home.

49

猴

HÓU

monkey

IN ancient times, skill in archery was the basis for selecting officials. In man (亻), precision in shooting an arrow (矢) at a target (厂 or コ) represented uprightness of heart. Hence the derived meaning of nobleman or prince: 侯. The addition of the animal radical: 犭 extends the meaning to: "Prince among animals," a title applicable to the noble monkey: 猴. Featured here is the King of Monkeys, legendary hero of the classic: "Journey to the West."

| ノ | 犭 | 犭 | 犭 | 犭 | 犭 | 犭 | 犭 | 犭 | 猴 | 猴 | | |

| 猴戏 | hóu xì | monkey show |
| 猴子 | hóu · zi | monkey |

Example

今 年 是 猴 年 。

Jīn nián shì hóu nián.

This is the year of the monkey.

50

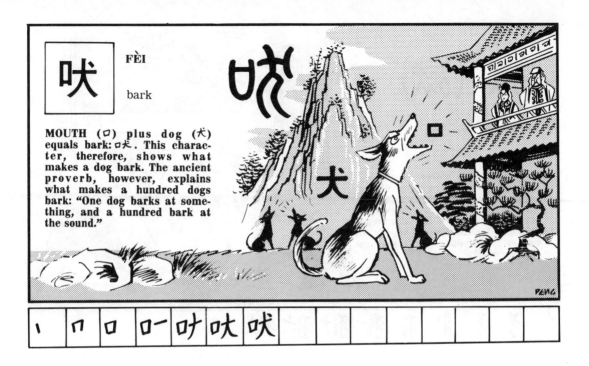

吠 FÈI

bark

MOUTH (口) plus dog (犬) equals bark: 吠. This character, therefore, shows what makes a dog bark. The ancient proverb, however, explains what makes a hundred dogs bark: "One dog barks at something, and a hundred bark at the sound."

丶 丨 口 口 吅 吠 吠

| 狗吠 | gǒu fèi | bark of dogs |
| 吠形吠声 | fèi xíng fèi shēng | to slavishly echo others — when one dog barks at a shadow, all the others join in |

Example

这 只 狗 的 吠 声 很 大 。
Zhè zhī gǒu · de fèi shēng hěn dà.
This dog barks very loudly.

51

獄 (獄)

YÙ prison; jail

THIS ideograph places speech (言) between two different forms of dogs (犭 and 犬). It represents a lawsuit: 獄, with the two suitors barking at each other like dogs. 獄 also means prison — for the loser. And, for the winner: "Win your lawsuit, and lose your money."

獄吏	yù lì	prison officer; jailer
獄卒	yù zú	prison guard
地獄	dì yù	hell
監獄	jiān yù	prison
入獄	rù yù	be imprisoned
越獄	yè yù	escape from prison

Example

他 因 被 判 有 罪 而 入 獄 。
Tā yīn bèi pàn yǒu zuì ér rù yù.

He was found guilty and sentenced to jail.

CHÒU

臭

stink

THE nose (自) of a dog (犬) is especially sensitive to smell. A dog (犬), therefore, that sticks out its nose (自) while personal business is being done suggests stench: 臭. By the same token, a person who sticks his nose into other people's personal business also stinks.

臭虫	chòu chóng	bedbug
臭骂	chòu mà	scold angrily and abusively
臭气	chòu qì	bad smell
臭味	chòu wèi	stink
臭鸡蛋	chòu jī dàn	rotten egg
臭名远扬	chòu míng yuǎn yáng	notorious
臭名昭著	chòu míng zhāo zhù	of ill repute; notorious
乳臭未干	rǔ chòu wèi gān	be young and inexperienced

Example

那 条 水 沟 臭 得 很 。
Nèi tiáo shuǐ gōu chòu dé hěn.
That drain stinks.

哭 KŪ
cry; wail; weep

THIS character uses two mouths (口口) to express intense action of the mouth, resembling the wailing of dogs (犬); so dog (犬) with two mouths (口口) means "wail": 哭. Two mouths may effectively express crying and howling, but certainly, "two buckets of tears," according to the proverb, "will not heal a bruise."

| 丶 | 冂 | 口 | 叮 | 叮口 | 口口 | 吅 | 哭 | 哭 | 哭 | | | |

哭泣	kū qì	cry; weep
哭诉	kū sù	complain tearfully
哭哭啼啼	kū kū tí tí	weep endlessly
哭丧着脸	kū sàng zhè liǎn	put on a long face
哭天抹泪	kū tiān mǒ lèi	wail and whine
哭笑不得	kū xiào bù dé	not knowing whether to laugh or to cry

Example

当 她 知 道 考 试 不 及 格 时 ， 便 哭 了 起 来 。
Dāng tā zhī dào kǎo shì bù jí gé shí, biàn kū · le qǐ lái.

When she knew she had failed the examinations, she burst into tears.

54

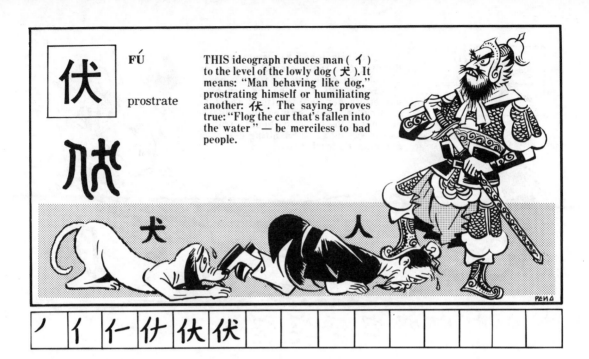

FÚ

prostrate

THIS ideograph reduces man (亻) to the level of the lowly dog (犬). It means: "Man behaving like dog," prostrating himself or humiliating another: 伏. The saying proves true: "Flog the cur that's fallen into the water" — be merciless to bad people.

犬　人

ノ　亻　仁　伏　伏　伏

伏安	fú ' ān	volt-ampere
伏兵	fú bīng	(troops in) ambush
伏法	fú fǎ	be executed
伏击	fú jī	ambush
伏流	fú liú	subterranean drainage; underground stream
伏贴	fú tiē	fit perfectly
伏尔加河	Fú ' Ěr Jiā Hé	the Volga (river)
伏特加酒	fú tè jiā jiǔ	vodka

Example

他　伏　在　地　上　不　动 。

Tā fú zài dì shàng bù dòng.

He lies face down on the ground, motionless.

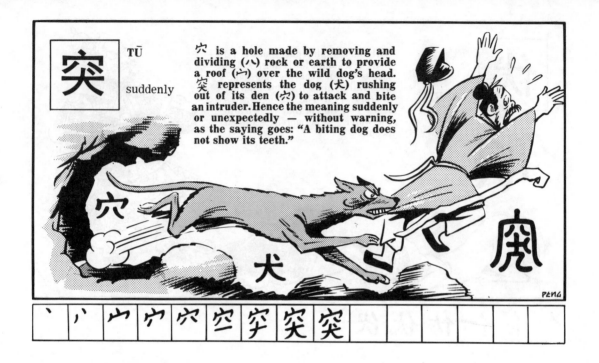

突 TŪ

suddenly

穴 is a hole made by removing and dividing (八) rock or earth to provide a roof (宀) over the wild dog's head. 突 represents the dog (犬) rushing out of its den (穴) to attack and bite an intruder. Hence the meaning suddenly or unexpectedly — without warning, as the saying goes: "A biting dog does not show its teeth."

丶 丷 宀 宀 穴 空 空 突 突

突变	tū biàn	sudden change	
突出	tū chū	protruding; outstanding	
突击	tū jī	a sudden and violent attack	
突破	tū pò	break through	
突起	tū qǐ	break out; rise high	

突然	tū rán	suddenly
突兀	tū wù	lofty (landscape); sudden
突袭	tū xí	surprise attack
突飞猛进	tū fēi měng jìn	advance by leaps and bounds
突如其来	tū rú qí lái	arise suddenly

Example

他 说 到 一 半 ， 突 然 停 了 。

Tā shuō dào yī bàn, tū rán tíng · le.

He was talking halfway when he stopped suddenly.

兽 (獸)

SHOÙ

animal; brute; beast

THE ancient form of 兽 graphically portrays the typical domestic animal with its ears, head, legs and tail. Clarified by the dog radical (犬), it means animals in general: 獸. The modern simplified form, however, discards the dog radical: 兽, even though sometimes a dog's life is to be preferred. In the words of the proverb: "Better a dog in times of peace than a man in times of war."

丶　丷　丷　屵　屵　由　由　兽　兽　兽　兽

兽环	shòu huán	door-knocker
兽类	shòu lèi	animals
兽王	shòu wáng	the king of beasts - the lion
兽行	shòu xíng	brutality
兽性	shòu xìng	barbarity

兽医	shòu yī	a vet
兽欲	shòu yù	animal desire
野兽	yě shòu	wild animal
兽力车	shòu lì chē	animal-drawn vehicle
人面兽心	rén miàn shòu xīn	a beast in human form

Example

在 非 洲 森 林 里 ， 有 许 多 野 兽 。
Zài Fēi Zhōu sēn lín lǐ, yǒu xǔ duō yě shòu.

There are many wild animals in the forests of Africa.

57

犹 (猶)

YÓU like; undecided

IN this extraordinary word, the phonetic: 酉 signifies liquor (酉) after fermentation, with the dregs settled or separated (八). Although its striking likeness to water may deceive even a dog (犭), its odour would cause hesitation and uncertainty. Hence it means both "like" and "undecided." 猶 is now simplified to 犹, the phonetic: 尤 meaning extraordinary. Because the dog reflects the image of its owner, "A lean dog shames its master."

ノ	犭	犭	犭	犭	犹	犹						

犹如	yóu rú	just as
犹疑	yóu yí	hesitate
犹豫	yóu yù	hesitate
犹太人	Yóu Tài rén	Jew

Example

他 做 事 常 常 犹 豫 不 决 。

Tā zuò shì cháng cháng yóu yù bù jué.

He often hesitates in whatever he does.

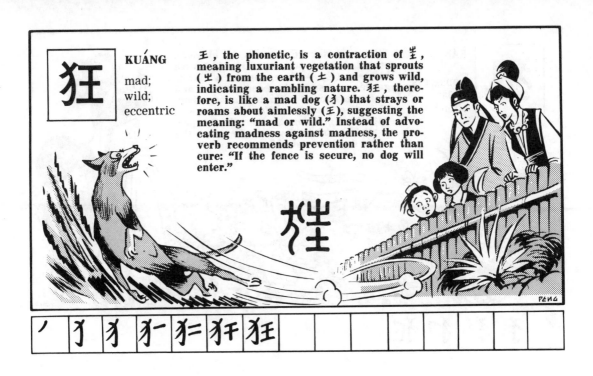

狂 KUÁNG

mad;
wild;
eccentric

王, the phonetic, is a contraction of 坒, meaning luxuriant vegetation that sprouts (坒) from the earth (土) and grows wild, indicating a rambling nature. 狂, therefore, is like a mad dog (犭) that strays or roams about aimlessly (王), suggesting the meaning: "mad or wild." Instead of advocating madness against madness, the proverb recommends prevention rather than cure: "If the fence is secure, no dog will enter."

狂暴	kuáng bào	violent	狂人	kuáng rén	maniac
狂放	kuáng fàng	unruly or unrestrained	狂喜	kuáng xǐ	wild with joy
狂吠	kuáng fèi	bark furiously	狂笑	kuáng xiào	laugh wildly
狂风	kuáng fēng	fierce wind	发狂	fā kuáng	mad
狂热	kuáng rè	fanaticism	狂想曲	kuáng xiǎng qǔ	rhapsody (music)

Example

昨 晚 的 一 场 狂 风 暴 雨 ， 把 许 多 树 吹 倒 了 。

Zuó wǎn‧de yī chǎng kuáng fēng bào yǔ, bǎ xǔ duō shù chuī dǎo‧le.

Many trees were crushed by yesterday's gale.

犯 FÀN

transgress;
violate;
offend

THE phonetic: 已 means to blossom, sprout, expand or erupt. Dog (犭) with blossom (已) — like dog in a flower garden — suggests heedlessness and transgression: 犯. Through miscarriage of justice, many an offender gets away with transgression; so laments the proverb: "The black dog eats the meat; the white dog is punished."

丿　犭　犭　犭　犯

犯法	fàn fǎ	violate the law	
犯规	fàn guī	break the rules	
犯忌	fàn jì	violate a taboo	
犯人	fàn rén	convict	
犯上	fàn shàng	go against one's superiors	

犯疑	fàn yí	suspect; be suspicious
犯罪	fàn zuì	commit a crime
战犯	zhàn fàn	war criminal
犯不着	fàn bù zháo	not worthwhile
杀人犯	shā rén fàn	murderer

Example

他 在 工 作 上 犯 了 错 误 。

Tā zài gōng zuò shàng fàn · le cuò wù.

He made a mistake in his work.

狠

HĚN

fierce;
vicious;
cruel

艮, the phonetic, is the classical abbreviation of 𦣻, made up of 目 (eye) and ㄴ (turn). It signifies to turn around and look a man defiantly in the face. With the addition of the dog radical (犭), indicating beastliness, it means: fierce, vicious, cruel or quarrelsome. But, concludes the proverb: "A good dog does not fight with chickens, nor a good man with his wife."

ノ 丿 犭 犭 犭 犭 狠 狠 狠

狠毒	hěn dú	vicious
狠心	hěn xīn	heartless
凶狠	xiōng hěn	ferocious and ruthless

Example

这 只 狮 子 很 凶 狠 。

Zhè zhǐ shī · zi hěn xiōng hěn.

This lion is ferocious.

LÁNG

wolf

THE wolf: 狼 has dog (犭) for radical. The phonetic: 良 was originally 畗 , modified to 畧 . 畗 signifies a gift (⊖) - godly nature, coming down from above (尸). 畧 , the modification, shows heaven and earth coming together (ㄚ) with the gift (⊖) eventually becoming lost (ㄴ). 狼 therefore suggests wolf - a dog that has lost its virtuous nature and acquired a vicious one. Hence the proverbial warning: "Outside he is clothed in a sheep's skin; inside his heart is a wolf's."

ノ 丨 犭 犭 犳 犲 犲 狠 狼 狼

狼狈	láng bèi	in an extremely awkward position
狼狗	láng gǒu	wolfhound
狼獾	láng huān	glutton
狼藉	láng jí	scattered about in a mess
豺狼	chái láng	jackal
狼狈为奸	láng bèi wéi jiān	act in collusion with each other
狼吞虎咽	láng tūn hǔ yàn	devour ravenously
狼心狗肺	láng xīn gǒu fèi	ungrateful; cruel and unscrupulous
狼子野心	láng zǐ yě xīn	wolfish nature; wild ambition

Example

我 方 兵 士 把 敌 人 打 得 十 分 狼 狈 。
Wǒ fāng bīng shì bǎ dí rén dǎ dé shí fēn láng bèi.
Our soldiers battered the enemy badly.

狮（獅）

SHĪ

lion

THE radical is the character for dog or beast (犭). The phonetic: 师 signifies the first (一) banner (巾) over the fort (𠂤), i.e., the banner of the commander-in-chief, and means: leader or master. Clarified by the dog radical (犭), the idea is set forth that the king or master (师) of beasts (犭) is the lion: 狮 .

狮子	shī · zi	lion
狮子狗	shī zǐ gǒu	pug-dog
狮子舞	shī zǐ wǔ	lion dance
狮子座	shī zǐ zuò	Leo (of the horoscope)

Example

新 加 坡 动 物 园 里 有 许 多 狮 子 。
Xīn Jiā Pō Dòng Wù Yuán lǐ yǒu xǔ duō shī · zi.

There are many lions in the Singapore Zoological Gardens.

猫（貓）

MĀO cat

THE radical: 豸 is a pictograph depicting a feline, a cat with its head, whiskers, paws and backbone. The older form: 貓 juxtaposes cat (豸) and sprout (苗) to denote that cats eat mice – destroyers of grain sprouts (艹) in the field (田). The enmity between cats and dogs is emphasised in the proverb: "If the dog goes when the cat comes, there will be no fight." However, in the modern form: 猫 , the cat (豸) goes when the dog (犭) comes."

| 丿 | 犭 | 犭 | 犭 | 犭 | 犭 | 犭 | 猫 | 猫 | 猫 | 猫 | | | |

小猫	xiǎo māo	kitten
雄猫	xióng māo	tom cat
熊猫	xióng māo	panda
猫头鹰	māo tóu yīng	owl
猫眼石	māo yǎn shí	cat's eye (mineral stone)

Example

这 只 小 猫 真 可 爱 。
Zhè zhī xiǎo māo zhēn kě ài.
This kitten is very lovable.

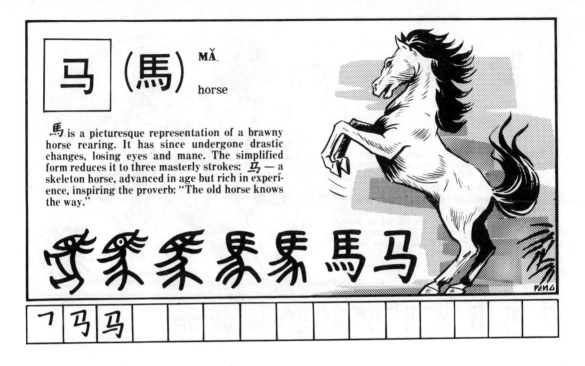

马 (馬) MǍ.

horse

馬 is a picturesque representation of a brawny horse rearing. It has since undergone drastic changes, losing eyes and mane. The simplified form reduces it to three masterly strokes: 马 — a skeleton horse, advanced in age but rich in experience, inspiring the proverb: "The old horse knows the way."

马鞍	mǎ' ān	saddle	马戏团	mǎ xì tuán	circus troupe
马鞭	mǎ biān	horsewhip	马拉松	mǎ lā sōng	marathon
马车	mǎ chē	horse-drawn carriage	马铃薯	mǎ líng shǔ	potato
马虎	mǎ hū	careless; casual	马不停蹄	mǎ bù tíng tí	nonstop
马上	mǎ shàng	at once; immediately	马到成功	mǎ dào chéng gōng	gain an immediate victory
马戏	mǎ xì	circus	马马虎虎	mǎ mǎ hū hū	careless; just passable

Example

马 儿 跑 得 快 。

Mǎ' ér pǎo dé kuài.

A horse runs very fast.

65

骑 （騎）

QÍ   ride; sit astride

THE phonetic 奇 means strange and wonderful. In association with 木 (wood) it forms 椅 (chair) — a wooden contraption, strange to those used to sitting on the floor. 馬 (horse) replaces 木 (wood) in the character for riding: 騎. To ride, therefore, is to sit on a horse （馬） — a wonderful （奇） experience. But don't get carried away too easily, warns the proverb: "The best riders are sure to fall."

| 乛 | 马 | 马 | 马 | 马⁺ | 马⁺ | 驴 | 驴 | 骑 | 骑 | 骑 | | |

骑兵	qí bīng	cavalryman
骑马	qí mǎ	ride a horse
骑士	qí shì	knight
骑术	qí shù	horsemanship

Example

那 将 军 骑 在 一 匹 白 马 上 。
Nà jiāng jūn qí zài yì pǐ bái mǎ shàng.

That general was riding on a white horse.

驯 (馴)

XÚN   tame; docile

THE concept of "tame" is derived by combining horse (馬) and river (川). Just as the flow of a river is controlled and guided by the land surface, so to tame (馴) is to subdue a horse (馬), guiding it like a river (川). Unfortunately, the treatment meted out to a tame horse is also applied to a good man. In the words of the proverb: "A good man is imposed upon just as a tame horse is ridden."

乛	马	马	马]	马川	马川							

驯服	xún fú	docile; tame
驯化	xún huà	domestication
驯良	xún liáng	tame and gentle
驯鹿	xún lù	reindeer
驯顺	xún shùn	tame and docile
驯养	xún yǎng	domesticate

Example

他 善 于 驯 虎 。

Tā shàn yú xún hǔ.

He is good at taming tigers.

67

骡 （騾） LUÓ
mule

THE phonetic 累 gives a clue to the identity of this member of the horse (馬) family. 累 was originally 畾, three articles (畾) connected or tied (糸) together, and means involved or accumulated, troublesome or unmanageable, burdened or tired. These traits characterise the mule: 騾, a beast of burden, noted for being stubborn. Its sluggishness prompts the saying: "A person riding a mule does not realise the slowness of walking."

骡夫	luó fū	a muleteer
骡马	luó mǎ	mules and horses
骡子	luó · zi	mule (the off-spring of an ass and a mare)
骡马店	luó mǎ diàn	an inn with sheds for carts and animals

Example

骡 子 可 以 拉 车 子 。
Luó · zi kě yǐ lā chē · zi.

Mules can draw carriages.

骆 （駱）

LUÒ camel

馬, representing a horse or beast of burden, is the radical. 各, the phonetic, means to go one's way unconcernedly, without heeding others. This is a dominant characteristic of the self-sufficient camel: 駱, an animal blessed with great endurance and ability to go without food and water for weeks.

骆驼	luò tuó	camel
骆驼队	luò tuó duì	camel train; caravan
骆驼绒	luò tuó róng	camel's hair material

Example

这 是 一 只 单 峰 骆 驼 。

Zhè shì yī zhī dān fēng luò tuó.

This is a one-humped camel.

闯 (闖)

CHUǍNG   rush; clash; charge

THE idea of rushing suddenly or rudely is graphically expressed in this ideograph of a swift horse (馬) dashing through a door (門). The character suggests rashness or impetuosity, something to guard against. As the proverb puts it: "When a word has left the lips, the swiftest horse cannot overtake it."

丶	丬	门	闩	闯	闯					

闯祸	chuǎng huò	get into trouble
闯将	chuǎng jiàng	daring general; path breaker
闯劲	chuǎng jìn	pioneering spirit
闯练	chuǎng liàn	leave home to temper oneself; be tempered in the world
闯江湖	chuǎng jiāng hú	make a living wandering from place to place (as a fortune-teller, acrobat, etc.)
横冲直闯	héng chōng zhí chuǎng	run amuck

Example

你 开 车 要 小 心 ， 千 万 别 闯 祸 。
Nǐ kāi chē yào xiǎo xīn, qiān wàn bié chuǎng huò.

Be careful with your driving and don't get into trouble.

70

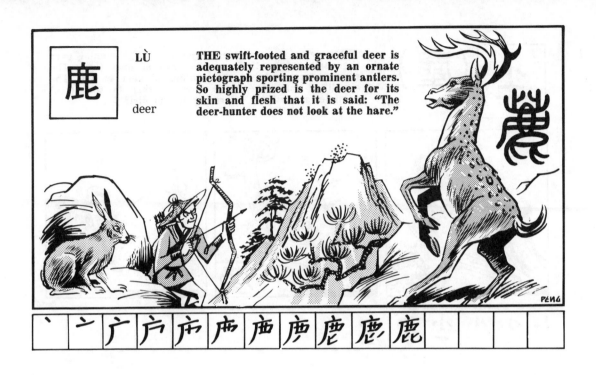

LÙ

鹿

deer

THE swift-footed and graceful deer is adequately represented by an ornate pictograph sporting prominent antlers. So highly prized is the deer for its skin and flesh that it is said: "The deer-hunter does not look at the hare."

丶　丶　广　广　产　产　产　鹿　鹿　鹿　鹿

鹿角	lù jiǎo	deerhorn; antler	鹿苑	lù yuàn	deer park
鹿圈	lù juàn	deer enclosure; deer pen	公鹿	gōng lù	buck
鹿皮	lù pí	deerskin	母鹿	mǔ lù	doe
鹿茸	lù róng	pilose antler	小鹿	xiǎo lù	fawn
鹿肉	lù ròu	venison	梅花鹿	méi huā lù	sika (deer)

Example

母 鹿 是 没 有 角 的 。
Mǔ lù shì méi yǒu jiǎo · de.
A doe has no antlers.

71

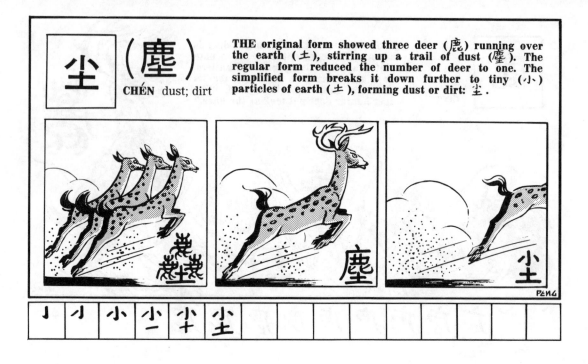

尘 (塵)

CHÉN dust; dirt

THE original form showed three deer (鹿) running over the earth (土), stirring up a trail of dust (塵). The regular form reduced the number of deer to one. The simplified form breaks it down further to tiny (小) particles of earth (土), forming dust or dirt: 尘.

尘埃	chén' āi	dust	尘世	chén shì	this world; this mortal life
尘暴	chén bào	dust storm	尘土	chén tǔ	dust
尘肺	chén fèi	pneumoconiosis	尘污	chén wū	soiled with dust
尘封	chén fēng	covered with dust; dust-laden	尘嚣	chén xiāo	hubbub; uproar
尘垢	chén gòu	dust and dirt	灰尘	huī chén	dust; dirt

Example

她 把 家 里 打 扫 得 一 尘 不 染 。

Tā bǎ jiā lǐ dǎ sǎo · de yī chén bù rǎn.

She kept the house spick and span.

庆 (慶)

QÌNG　celebrate; congratulate

IN ancient times it was traditional to go (夂) and offer, on a festive day, a deer's (鹿) skin with hearty (心) wishes. Hence: 慶, to celebrate, congratulate or bring a blessing. The simplified form for celebration puts it in a nutshell: something big (大) under cover or roof (广) — a big occasion indoors.

丶	宀	广	广	庁	庆						

庆典	qìng diǎn	celebration
庆贺	qìng hè	celebrate
庆幸	qìng xìng	rejoice
庆祝	qìng zhù	celebrate
庆功会	qìng gōng huì	victory meeting
国庆日	guó qìng rì	National Day

Example

八 月 九 日 是 我 国 的 国 庆 日 。
Bā yuè jiǔ rì shì wǒ guó·de guó qìng rì.
Our National Day falls on August 9.

丽 （麗）

LÌ beautiful; handsome; elegant

THIS character for beauty and elegance is a picture of the graceful deer (鹿) decorated with a pair of pendants (丽). The simplified form displays the pair of pendants linked together: 丽. Physical attractiveness is not to be envied, if we go by the saying: "Beautiful women generally suffer an evil fate; intelligent young men are seldom handsome."

一	厂	兀	丙	丙	丽	丽							

丽人	lì rén	a beauty
美丽	měi lì	beautiful
风和日丽	fēng hé rì lì	lovely weather

Example

雪 山 的 风 景 真 美 丽 ！
Xuě shān · de fēng jǐng zhēn měi lì!

The scenery of snow-clad mountains is lovely.

74

HŬ

tiger

THE character for tiger is a pictograph. It is based on the radical 虍 (tiger skin) clarified by 几 (hind legs): 虎. Characterised by its vicious ferocity, the tiger strikes fear even when dead. Hence the saying: "He who rides the tiger finds it difficult to dismount." (骑虎难下)

丨	广	上	卢	卢	虍	虏	虎						

虎伏	hǔ fú	gyro wheel	虎穴	hǔ xué	tiger's den
虎将	hǔ jiàng	brave general	老虎	lǎo hǔ	tiger
虎劲	hǔ jìn	dauntless drive; dash	虎视耽耽	hǔ shì dān dān	eye covetously
虎口	hǔ kǒu	tiger's mouth — jaws of death	虎头蛇尾	hǔ tóu shé wěi	fine start and poor finish
虎钳	hǔ qián	vice	马马虎虎	mǎ mǎ hū hū	careless; fair

Example

老 虎 是 肉 食 动 物 。
Lǎo hǔ shì ròu shí dòng wù.

The tiger is a carnivore.

号 (號)

HÁO shout
HÀO mark; number

号 comes from mouth (口) uttering an exclamation (丂, the breath 丂 rising against an obstacle 一). 号 therefore means to cry out. The presence of the tiger (虎) gives the needed impetus to shout: 號. In the simplified form, the tiger is eliminated: 号. 號 also means mark or number, usually announced by the mouth, with a call or cry.

| 一 | 口 | 口 | 므 | 号 | | | | | | | |

号哭	háo kū	wail	号召	hào zhào	call; appeal
号叫	háo jiào	howl; yell	编号	biān hào	serial number
号称	hào chēng	known as; claim to be	绰号	chuò hào	nickname
号令	hào lìng	order	问号	wèn hào	question mark
号码	hào mǎ	number	号啕大哭	háo táo dà kū	cry one's eyes out

Example

请 问 你 的 电 话 几 号 ?
Qǐng wèn nǐ · de diàn huà jǐ hào?

What is your telephone number?

76

XIÀNG elephant

THIS character is a striking image of the elephant, emphasising its trunk and precious tusks: 象. Valuable possessions can pose a hazard to life; in the words of the proverb: "The elephant is killed because of its tusks."

丶 ⺈ ⺈ ⺈ 乀 乀 刍 争 象 象 象 象

象鼻	xiàng bí	trunk (of an elephant)	
象棋	xiàng qí	Chinese chess	
象散	xiàng sàn	astigmatism	
象声	xiàng shēng	onomatopoeia	
象限	xiàng xiàn	quadrant	

象牙	xiàng yá	elephant's tusk; ivory
象样	xiàng yàng	presentable
象征	xiàng zhēng	symbolise; signify
好象	hǎo xiàng	seem; like
象牙雕刻	xiàng yá diāo kè	ivory carving

Example

这 个 象 牙 雕 刻 很 精 致 。
Zhè gè xiàng yá diāo kè hěn jīng zhì.

This is an exquisite ivory carving.

XIÀNG

portrait; image

IN THIS character the phonetic 象 means elephant and also image. The radical 亻 (man) clarifies its application to man and means image, portrait or resemblance: 像 Man has been making images of everything imaginable under and above the sun. So, reasons the proverb: "No image-maker worships the gods; he knows what they are made of."

丿 亻 亻 伫 伫 伊 俏 侉 侉 侉 俊 像 像 像

像样	xiàng yàng	up to the mark; presentable; decent
像话	xiàng huà	reasonable; proper; right
人像	rén xiàng	portrait; image

Example

这 位 画 家 画 的 人 像 很 逼 真 。
Zhè wèi huà jiā huà·de rén xiàng hěn bī zhēn.

This artist's portraits are very realistic.

熊 XÍONG

bear

熊 is a representation of the bear, with its head (厶), hairy body (月) and paws (匕). The bear is a symbol of bravery, and is extremely strong and able. Hence: 能, meaning able. To differentiate bear from ability (能) four dots (灬) standing for feet are added: 熊.

厶 厶 广 牟 牟 能 能 能 能 能 能 能

熊蜂	xióng fēng	bumble bee
熊猴	xióng hóu	Assamese macaque
熊猫	xióng māo	panda
熊掌	xióng zhǎng	bear's claw (as a rare delicacy)
狗熊	gǒu xióng	Asiatic black bear
熊熊大火	xióng xióng dà huǒ	raging fire

Example

熊 猫 是 惹 人 喜 爱 的 动 物 。

Xióng māo shì rě rén xǐ ài · de dòng wù.

Pandas are lovable animals.

兔 is a pictograph of the squatting hare or rabbit, with its tail perked up. Noted for its shrewdness in the struggle for survival, the proverbial hare has three holes to its burrow — and it does not eat the grass around it.

TÙ

hare; rabbit

兔狲	tù sūn	steppe cat
兔脱	tù tuō	run away like a hare; escape; flee
兔子	tù · zi	rabbit; hare
白兔	bái tù	white rabbit
兔死狗烹	tù sǐ gǒu pēng	trusted aides are eliminated when they have outlived their usefulness

Example

兔 子 爱 吃 萝 卜 。
Tù · zi ài chī luó · bo.

Rabbits love carrots.

YUĀN

oppression;
injustice

AN inoffensive hare (兔) confined under a cover (冖) suggests oppression: 冤. By extension, 冤 also means injustice and false accusation. Oppression has long established itself in human society but, asserts the proverb: "A house established by oppression cannot long enjoy prosperity."

冤仇	yuān chóu	enmity
冤家	yuān jiā	foe; enemy
冤屈	yuān qū	wrongful treatment
冤头	yuān‧tou	enemy; foe
冤枉	yuān‧wang	treat unjustly
冤狱	yuān yù	an unjust charge or verdict; a miscarriage of justice; frame-up
冤家路窄	yuān jiā lù zhǎi	one can't avoid one's enemy
冤有头，	yuān yǒu tóu,	every injustice has its perpetrator, every debt has its debtor
债有主	zhài yǒu zhǔ	

Example

他 们 俩 是 冤 家 ， 常 因 小 事 反 脸 。

Tā‧men liǎng shì yuān jiā, cháng yīn xiǎo shì fǎn liǎn.

The two of them are enemies and always quarrel at the slightest thing.

逸　**YÌ**

escape;
leisure

THE radical 辶 means to go fast and stop suddenly. Combined with 兔 (rabbit), it suggests a rabbit on the run, and means to flee, escape or retire from the world. The hare, being regarded as a profligate, 逸 also means to lead an idle and licentious life.

ノ　ク　ク　ク　ケ　免　兔　兔　兔　逸　逸

逸乐	yì lè	comfort and pleasure
逸民	yì mín	hermit (in ancient times); recluse
逸事	yì shì	anecdote (especially about famous people)
逸闻	yì wén	anecdote
逃逸	táo yì	escape
好逸恶劳	hào yì wù láo	love ease and hate work

Example

年 青 人 千 万 不 可 好 逸 恶 劳 。

Nián qīng rén qiān wàn bù kě hào yì wù láo.

Young people must not love ease and hate work.

82

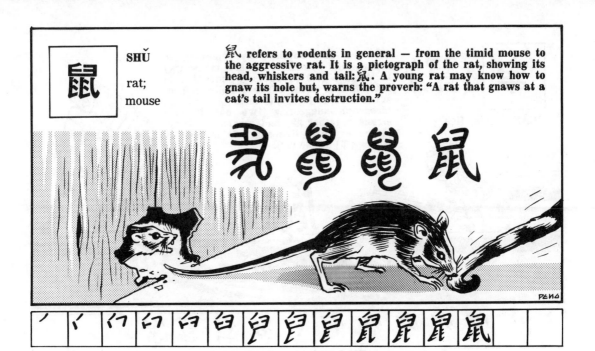

| 鼠 | SHǓ rat; mouse | 鼠 refers to rodents in general — from the timid mouse to the aggressive rat. It is a pictograph of the rat, showing its head, whiskers and tail: 鼠. A young rat may know how to gnaw its hole but, warns the proverb: "A rat that gnaws at a cat's tail invites destruction." |

鼠辈	shǔ bèi	scoundrels
鼠疫	shǔ yì	plague
老鼠	lǎo shǔ	mouse; rat
老鼠过街，	lǎo shǔ guò jiē,	when a rat runs across the street, everybody cries, "Kill it!" (said of a
人人喊打	rén rén hǎn dǎ	person or thing hated by everyone)

Example

老 鼠 是 惹 人 讨 厌 的 动 物 。

Lǎo shǔ shì rě rén tǎo yàn·de dòng wù.

Mice are hateful creatures.

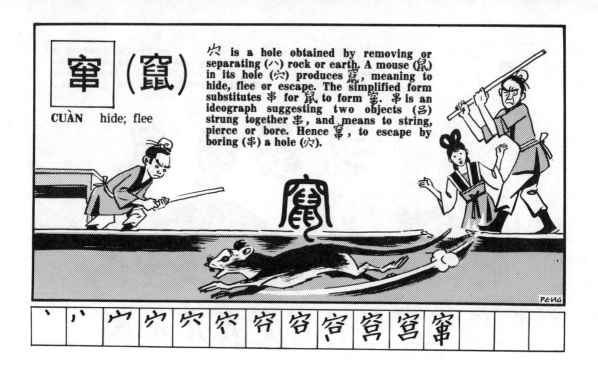

窜 (竄)

CUÀN   hide; flee

穴 is a hole obtained by removing or separating (八) rock or earth. A mouse (鼠) in its hole (穴) produces 竄, meaning to hide, flee or escape. The simplified form substitutes 串 for 鼠 to form 窜. 串 is an ideograph suggesting two objects (吕) strung together 串, and means to string, pierce or bore. Hence 窜, to escape by boring (串) a hole (穴).

丶 八 宀 灾 灾 穴 容 容 窀 窀 窝 窜

窜犯　　　cuàn fàn　　　raid; make an inroad into
窜改　　　cuàn gǎi　　　tamper with; alter
窜扰　　　cuàn rǎo　　　harass
窜逃　　　cuàn táo　　　flee in disorder
鼠窜　　　shǔ cuàn　　　scurry like rats
东逃西窜　dōng táo xī cuàn　flee in all directions

Example

学 生 们 看 到 校 长 都 东 逃 西 窜 。
Xué shēng·men kàn dào xiào zhǎng dōu dōng táo xī cuàn.

The students fled in all directions at the sight of their principal.

84

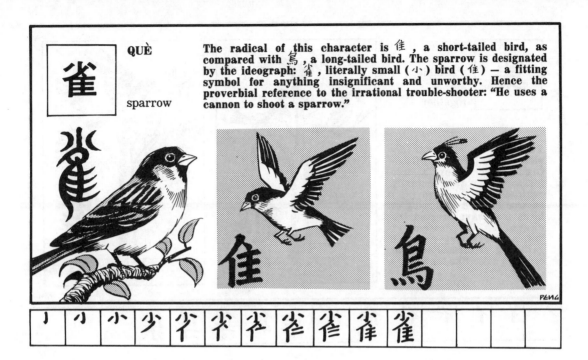

QUÈ

雀

sparrow

The radical of this character is 隹, a short-tailed bird, as compared with 鳥, a long-tailed bird. The sparrow is designated by the ideograph: 雀, literally small (小) bird (隹) — a fitting symbol for anything insignificant and unworthy. Hence the proverbial reference to the irrational trouble-shooter: "He uses a cannon to shoot a sparrow."

雀斑	què bān	freckle
雀鲷	què diāo	damselfish
雀鹰	què yīng	sparrow hawk
雀跃	què yuè	jump for joy
麻雀	má què	sparrow

Example

他 的 脸 上 有 很 多 雀 斑 。
Tā · de liǎn shàng yǒu hěn duō què bān.

He has a freckled face.

85

集 JÍ
assemble;
gather
together

The ancient character depicted three birds (雥) flocking together atop a tree (木). This was eventually contracted to 集 : bird (隹) on tree (木). A gathering of birds may have created the character for "assembly" but, as the saying goes: "A gathering of mosquitoes can create a noise like thunder."

ノ 亻 亻 仁 仁 佳 佳 隹 隼 隼 集

集合	jí hé	gather		集团	jí tuán	group; bloc
集会	jí huì	assembly		集训	jí xùn	centralised training
集锦	jí jǐn	a collection of choice specimens		集邮	jí yóu	stamp-collecting
				集中	jí zhōng	concentrate
集市	jí shì	country fair; market		聚集	jù jí	gather
集体	jí tǐ	collective				

Example

大 门 口 聚 集 了 一 大 堆 人 。
Dà mén kǒu jù jí · le yī dà duī rén.
A big crowd gathered at the gate.

只（隻）

ZHĪ　one; single

A bird (隹) in hand (又) means "one" or "single": 隻 and is used as a numerative or classifier for birds, animals, ships and single individuals of things in pairs or sets, as arm, eye, hand, shoe, etc. It is now replaced by the simplified form: 只 , which, incidentally, means "only."

丶	冂	口	尸	只									

只身	zhī shēn	alone; by oneself
一只	yī zhī	used as a numerative or classifier
只言片语	zhī yán piàn yǔ	a word or two

Example

他 只 身 前 往 外 国 。
Tā　zhī　shēn　qián　wǎng　wài　guó.

He goes abroad alone.

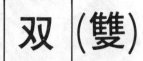

SHUĀNG　　a pair

Just as one bird (隹) in hand (又) means single: 隻, so two birds (隹隹) in hand (又) stand for a pair: 雙. The simplified form shows just two hands: 双 — a clearer representation because hands, unlike birds, always come in pairs. Unfortunately, according to the saying, "Blessings never come in pairs, nor misfortunes singly."

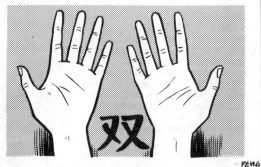

フ	又	邓	双									

双边	shuāng biān	bilateral	双生	shuāng shēng	twin
双层	shuāng céng	double-deck; two layers	双喜	shuāng xǐ	double happiness
			双月刊	shuāng yuè kān	bi-monthly
双重	shuāng chóng	double	双周刊	shuāng zhōu kān	bi-weekly
双方	shuāng fāng	both sides	双管齐下	shuāng guǎn qí xià	work along both lines
双亲	shuāng qīn	(both) parents			

Example

他 买 了 一 双 新 鞋 。
Tā mǎi·le yī shuāng xīn xié.
He bought a new pair of shoes.

进 (進)

JÌN advance; enter

This character is made up of "move" (辶, contraction of 辵) and "bird" (隹). When birds "move" they always fly forward, never backward. So 進 means to "advance." In the simplified form, 井 (order) replaces 隹 (bird), suggesting advancement and, by extension, entry: 进 — an orderly movement encouraged by the proverb: "He who does not advance loses ground" (不進則退).

一 二 弍 井 井 进 进

进步	jìn bù	progress; advance	进食	jìn shí	have one's meal
进度	jìn dù	rate of progress	进行	jìn xíng	be in progress
进攻	jìn gōng	attack	进展	jìn zhǎn	make progress
进化	jìn huà	evolution	进出口	jìn chū kǒu	import and export
进取(心)	jìn qǔ (xīn)	enterprising (spirit)	进一步	jìn yī bù	go a step further

Example

你 的 华 语 大 有 进 步 了 。
Nǐ · de Huá yǔ dà yǒu jìn bù · le.

Your Chinese has improved.

售 SHÒU

sell

The original ideograph for "sell" represented two birds (雔), the buyer and the seller, haggling with the mouth (口). The modern character shows only one bird (隹), the seller, marketing his wares with the mouth (口). The proverb explains the absence of the buyer: "Fuel is not sold in the forest, nor fish on the shore of the lake."

ノ 亻 亻 仁 仁 仹 隹 隹 隹 售

售货	shòu huò	sell goods
售价	shòu jià	selling price
售卖	shòu mài	sell
出售	chū shòu	offer for sale
售票处	shòu piào chù	ticket office
售票口	shòu piào kǒu	wicket
售票员	shòu piào yuán	ticket seller; conductor
女售货员	nǚ shòu huò yuán	salesgirl

Example

这 餐 具 的 售 价 是 一 千 五 百 元 。

Zhè cān jù ·de shòu jià shì yī qiān wǔ bǎi yuán.

The selling price of this dinner set is $1,500.

90

JIĀO

焦

burnt; scorched

Bird (隹) over fire (灬) means "burnt or scorched": 焦, and by extension, "worried or anxious." Man has always felt like a bird over fire. In the words of the saying: "One does not live a hundred years, yet worries enough for a thousand."

ノ 亻 亻 亻 仁 仁 住 住 隹 隹 隹 焦

焦点	jiāo diǎn	focal point	
焦化	jiāo huà	coking	
焦黄	jiāo huáng	sallow; brown	
焦急	jiāo jí	anxious	
焦距	jiāo jù	focal distance; focal length	

焦渴	jiāo kě	terribly thirsty; parched
焦虑	jiāo lǜ	feel anxious
焦炭	jiāo tàn	coke
焦土	jiāo tǔ	scorched earth – ravages of war
焦头烂额	jiāo tóu làn´é	badly battered; in a terrible fix

Example

这 块 饼 被 烤 焦 了 。
Zhè kuài bǐng bèi kǎo jiāo·le.

This piece of biscuit is burnt.

91

难 (難)

NÁN difficult; not easy

The phonetic 菓 is a contraction of yellow (黄) earth (土) — clay dried in the sun and therefore barren. The addition of bird (隹) as radical suggests the plight of birds living in such an environment. Hence: 難, signifying difficulty or distress. The simplified form: 难 conveys the idea even more forcefully: a bird (隹) firmly grasped in the hand (又).

丁	又	矛	矛	矛	丬	丬	丬	难	难

难倒	nán dǎo	daunt	难看	nán kàn	ugly
难得	nán dé	hard to come by; rare	难受	nán shòu	feel unwell
难怪	nán guài	no wonder	难忘	nán wàng	unforgettable
难过	nán guò	have a hard time; be grieved	难为情	nán wéi qíng	ashamed; shy
难堪	nán kān	intolerable; embarrassed	难言之隐	nán yán zhī yǐn	something which would be awkward to disclose

Example

这 条 路 很 难 走 。

Zhè tiáo lù hěn nán zǒu.

This road is difficult to pass.

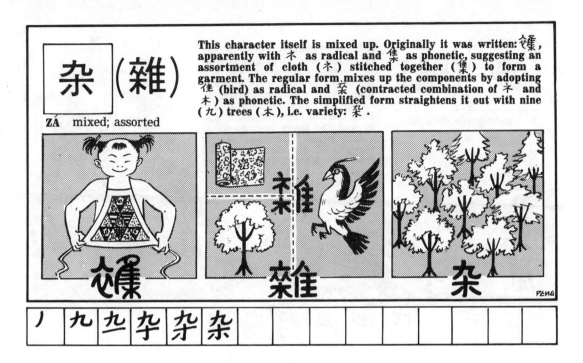

ZÁ mixed; assorted

This character itself is mixed up. Originally it was written: 襍, apparently with 衤 as radical and 集 as phonetic, suggesting an assortment of cloth (衤) stitched together (集) to form a garment. The regular form mixes up the components by adopting 隹 (bird) as radical and 枀 (contracted combination of 衤 and 木) as phonetic. The simplified form straightens it out with nine (九) trees (木), i.e. variety: 杂.

杂草	zá cǎo	weeds	杂务	zá wù	sundry duties
杂费	zá fèi	sundry fees	杂志	zá zhì	magazine
杂货	zá huò	groceries	夹杂	jiā zá	mingled; mixed
杂技	zá jì	acrobatics	杂而不乱	zá ér bù luàn	mixed but not confused
杂乱	zá luàn	in a jumble	杂乱无章	zá luàn wú zhāng	disorderly and unsystematic

Example

这 花 盆 长 满 了 杂 草 。
Zhè huā péng zhǎng mǎn·le zá cǎo.
This flower pot is full of weeds.

93

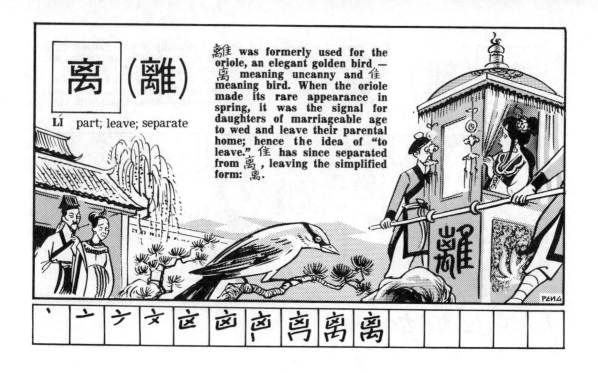

离 (離)

Lí   part; leave; separate

離 was formerly used for the oriole, an elegant golden bird — 离 meaning uncanny and 隹 meaning bird. When the oriole made its rare appearance in spring, it was the signal for daughters of marriageable age to wed and leave their parental home; hence the idea of "to leave." 隹 has since separated from 离, leaving the simplified form: 离.

离别	lí bié	part; bid farewell
离婚	lí hūn	divorce
离间	lí jiàn	sow discord
离境	lí jìng	leave a country or place
离开	lí kāi	leave; depart from; deviate from

离奇	lí qí	odd; fantastic
离题	lí tí	stray from the subject
距离	jù lí	distance
离乡背井	lí xiāng bèi jǐng	leave one's native place
离群索居	lí qún suǒ jū	live in solitude

Example

她 离 家 已 经 三 年 了 。

Tā lí jiā yǐ jīng sān nián · le.

She's been away from home for three years.

鸡 (鷄)

JĪ chicken

THE radical 鳥 stands for bird. The phonetic 奚 signifies an adult (大) with hand (爪 or 爫) on silk thread (糸 or 纟) — a spinner. Previously, women prisoners were condemned to spinning without getting any benefit, not unlike the chicken confined to the labour of laying eggs for its owner. A bird (鸟) in hand (又) produces the simplified chicken: 鸡 , a really handy bird.

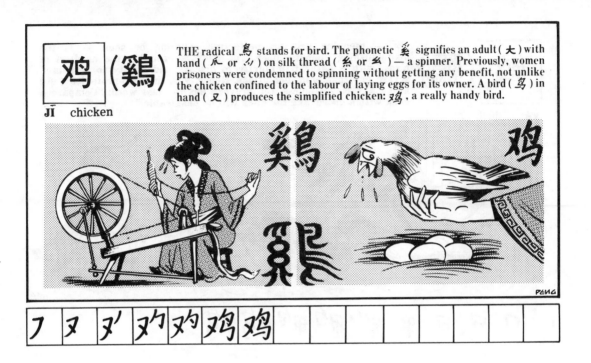

鸡蛋	jī dàn	chicken's egg	鸡皮疙瘩	jī pí gē·da	goose flesh
鸡毛	jī máo	chicken's feather	鸡犬不宁	jī quǎn bù níng	even fowls and dogs are not left in peace — (fig.) general turmoil
鸡肉	jī ròu	meat of chicken			
公鸡	gōng jī	cock; rooster			
母鸡	mǔ jī	hen	鸡尾酒会	jī wěi jiǔ huì	cocktail party
鸡蛋糕	jī dàn gāo	sponge cake	鸡蛋里挑骨头	jī dàn lǐ tiāo gǔ tóu	look for a bone in an egg — (fig.) find fault

Example

这些 鸡蛋 不 新鲜 ， 不 可以 吃 。

Zhè xiē jī dàn bù xīn xiān, bù kě yǐ chī.

These eggs are not fresh, they cannot be eaten.

鸭 (鴨)

YĀ duck

甲 — meaning armour, protective covering or shell — is the distinguishing phonetic here. The duck is probably the hardiest of birds, with a natural immunity to disease and ability to withstand severe environmental conditions. Hence: 鴨, the well-protected (甲) bird (鳥). Nevertheless, the proverb has the last word: "Compare a duck with a goose, and the duck will be unsaleable."

| 丨 | 冂 | 冃 | 日 | 甲 | 甲′ | 甲丿 | 甲勹 | 鸭 | 鸭 | | | | |

鸭蛋	yā dàn	duck's egg
鸭绒	yā róng	duck's down; eiderdown
公鸭	gōng yā	drake
母鸭	mǔ yā	duck
小鸭	xiǎo yā	duckling
鸭舌帽	yā shé mào	peaked cap
鸭嘴笔	yā zuǐ bǐ	drawing pen; ruling pen
鸭嘴兽	yā zuǐ shòu	platypus; duckbill

Example

你 吃 过 北 京 鸭 吗 ?

Nǐ chī guò Běi Jīng yā · ma?

Have you tried Beijing duck?

96

鸽 (鴿)

GĒ dove; pigeon

合 indicates harmony of many (亼) mouths (口), 亼 symbolising unity and agreement of three lines forming a balanced triangle. 鴿 ideographically refers to the dove or pigeon — the bird (鳥) that flocks together in peace, harmony and unity (合).

丿 亻 仒 仐 合 合 合' 台勹 台勹 鸽 鸽

鸽子	gē · zi	pigeon; dove
家鸽	jiā gē	domestic pigeon
野鸽	yě gē	wild pigeon
鸽子笼	gē · zi lóng	pigeon cote

Example

在 伦 敦 的 特 拉 法 广 场 有 许 多 鸽 子 。
Zài Lún Dūn · de Tè Lā Fǎ guǎng chǎng yǒu xǔ duō gē · zi.

There are many pigeons at the Trafalgar Square in London.

凤 （鳳）

FÈNG   phoenix (male)

ORIGINALLY, the phoenix was represented by 网 (朋), its tail. As it flew, it drew all birds to it in friendship. Eventually 朋 became a symbol of friendship, and a new character was adopted for the phoenix: 鳳 — a pictograph of the bird — relating it to wind （風） in sound and symbol. The simplified form substitutes a friendly hand （又） for the friendly phoenix: 凤.

| 丿 | 几 | 凡 | 凤 | | | | | | | | |

凤凰	fèng huáng	phoenix
凤梨	fèng lí	pineapple
凤尾鱼	fèng wěi yú	anchovy
凤尾竹	fèng wěi zhú	fernleaf hedge bamboo
凤仙花	fèng xiān huā	balsam plant
凤毛麟角	fèng máo lín jiǎo	phoenix feathers and unicorn horns — (fig.) rarity of rarities

Example

她 的 衣 服 上 绣 有 一 只 凤 凰 。
Tā · de yī fú shàng xiù yǒu yī zhī fèng huáng.

There is a phoenix embroidered on her dress.

YÀN swallow

燕 is a symmetrical pictograph of the swallow flying upwards. Swallows abound in the northern hemisphere and are always a welcome sight in spring. The swallow (燕) is fondly remembered as a bird from the north (北), flying across the waters (灬) with a stalk (一) of grass (艹) in its mouth (口).

燕麦	yàn mài	oats
燕鸥	yàn ' ōu	tern
燕隼	yàn sǔn	hobby
燕窝	yàn wō	edible bird's nest
燕鱼	yàn yú	Spanish mackerel
燕子	yàn · zi	swallow
燕尾服	yàn wěi fú	tuxedo

Example

燕　窝　是　一　种　珍　贵　的　食　品　。
Yàn　wō　shì　yī　zhǒng　zhēn　guì·de　shí　pǐn.

Bird's nest is a valuable delicacy.

99

不 BÙ

not

THIS character represents a bird flying up towards the sky and disappearing from sight, as if becoming non-existent. The horizontal stroke (一) signifies the sky as the limit, blocking the bird (小) from ever reaching its destination. Hence the idea of "not", a negative: 不. Arrogant man, unable even to walk with his fellowman, now tries to fly; to him also, the sky is the limit.

一 ㄱ 不 不

不安	bù ' ān	uneasy; disturbed	
不便	bù biàn	inconvenient	
不断	bù duàn	continuous	
不顾	bù gù	in spite of; regardless of	
不得已	bù dé yǐ	act against one's will	

不客气	bù kè·qi	impolite
不辞而别	bù cí ér bié	leave without saying goodbye
不得人心	bù dé rén xīn	be unpopular
不怀好意	bù huái hǎo yì	harbour evil designs
不欢而散	bù huān ér sàn	break up in discord

Example

社 会 是 在 不 断 地 进 步 中 。
Shè huì shì zài bù duàn·di jìn bù zhōng.
Society is constantly making progress.

WĀI

crooked

歪 is an ideograph composed of two characters: 不 (not) and 正 (upright). It means: not straight, i.e., crooked. 正 itself indicates stopping (止) at a line or limit (一), without going astray, hence upright. Although imperfect, we do well to heed the proverbial counsel: "Stand upright, and don't worry if your shadow is crooked."

| 一 | ブ | 才 | 不 | 歪 | 歪 | 歪 | 歪 | 歪 | | | | |

歪风	wāi fēng	unhealthy trend
歪曲	wāi qū	distort; misrepresent
歪诗	wāi shī	inelegant verses; doggerel
歪斜	wāi xié	crooked
歪歪扭扭	wāi wāi niǔ niǔ	crooked; askew; shapeless and twisted
邪门歪道	xié mén wāi dào	crooked ways; dishonest practices

Example

这 堵 墙 有 点 歪 。
Zhè dǔ qiáng yǒu diǎn wāi.

This wall is a little tilted.

ZHÌ

arrive; reach

THE character 至 is the opposite of 不 which represents a bird flying straight upwards but unable to reach its destination. The original form 𝕪 is a pictograph of a bird, bending its wings and darting downwards to the earth and reaching it. 至 is the modern form, meaning: arrive or reach.

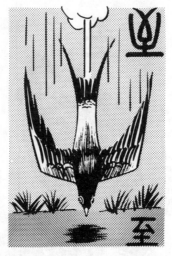

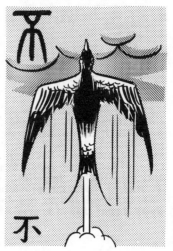

PENG

| 一 | 工 | 互 | 丞 | 至 | 至 | | | | | | | | |

至诚	zhì chéng	utmost sincerity	至少	zhì shǎo	at the least
至多	zhì duō	at the most	至死	zhì sǐ	till death
至交	zhì jiāo	most intimate friend	至于	zhì yú	as for; as to
至今	zhì jīn	up to now; so far	至高无上	zhì gāo wú shàng	most lofty; supreme
至上	zhì shàng	supreme; the highest	至理名言	zhì lǐ míng yán	maxim; famous dictum

Example

我 至 今 还 未 得 到 他 的 答 复 。

Wǒ zhì jīn hái wèi dé dào tā ·de dá fù.

So far, I've had no reply from him yet.

102

屋

WŪ house

THE phonetic 至 means to arrive or reach, and the radical 尸 is a reclining figure. 屋 is where you recline (尸) on arrival (至) — a place of rest, a house. And a house, once built, is permanently at rest; hence the saying: "Before you build a house, know your neighbourhood."

屋顶	wū dǐng	roof
屋脊	wū jǐ	ridge (of a roof)
屋架	wū jià	roof truss
屋檐	wū yán	eaves
屋宇	wū yǔ	house
屋子	wū·zi	dwelling place
瓦屋面	wǎ wū miàn	tile roofing
世界屋脊	shì jiè wū jǐ	the roof of the world (The Himalayas)

Example

她 的 屋 子 后 面 有 个 大 花 园 。

Tā · de wū · zi hòu miàn yǒu gè dà huā yuán.

There is a big garden behind her house.

103

室 **SHÌ**
room; chamber

THE ideograph 室 suggests arrival (至) at a destination under a roof (宀), i.e., a room enclosed by walls. And because there are two sides to the wall, "One family builds a wall, two families enjoy it."

丶 丷 宀 宀 宀 宀 宀 宀 室

室外	shì wài	outdoor
课室	kè shì	classroom
卧室	wò shì	bedroom
办公室	bàn gōng shì	office
会客室	huì kè shì	reception room
室内设计	shì nèi shè jì	interior designing
室内装饰	shì nèi zhuāng shì	interior decorating

Example

他 把 一 架 电 视 机 放 在 卧 室 里 。
Tā bǎ yī jià diàn shì jī fàng zài wò shì lǐ.

He put a TV set in his bedroom.

龟 (龜)

GUĪ

tortoise

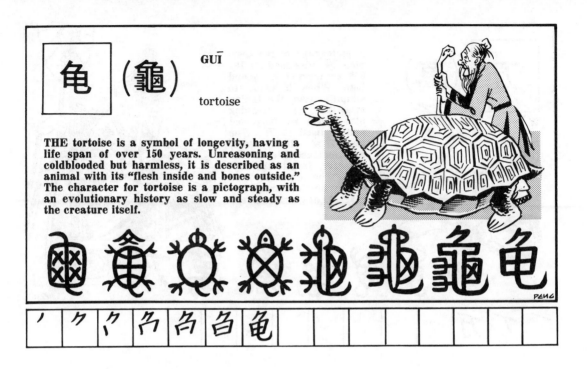

THE tortoise is a symbol of longevity, having a life span of over 150 years. Unreasoning and coldblooded but harmless, it is described as an animal with its "flesh inside and bones outside." The character for tortoise is a pictograph, with an evolutionary history as slow and steady as the creature itself.

龟板	guī bǎn	tortoise plastron
龟背	guī bèi	curvature of the spinal column
龟甲	guī jiǎ	tortoise-shell
龟缩	guī suō	withdraw into passive defence
乌龟	wū guī	tortoise

Example

乌 龟 的 寿 命 很 长 。

Wū guī·de ‚shòu mìng hěn cháng.

The tortoise has a long life-span.

105

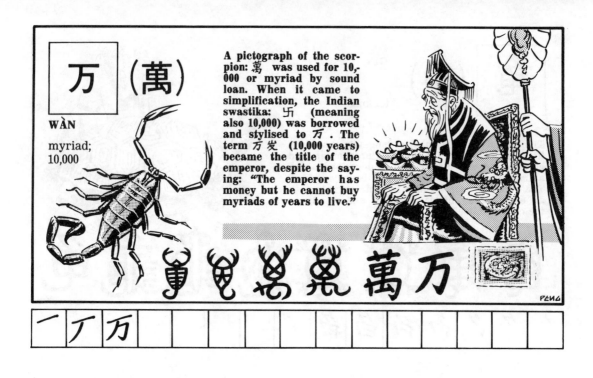

万 (萬)

WÀN

myriad;
10,000

A pictograph of the scorpion: 萬 was used for 10,-000 or myriad by sound loan. When it came to simplification, the Indian swastika: 卐 (meaning also 10,000) was borrowed and stylised to 万. The term 万岁 (10,000 years) became the title of the emperor, despite the saying: "The emperor has money but he cannot buy myriads of years to live."

万般	wàn bān	all the different kinds	万事	wàn shì	all things
万端	wàn duān	multifarious	万一	wàn yī	just in case
万分	wàn fēn	very much; extremely	万丈	wàn zhàng	lofty or bottomless
万古	wàn gǔ	eternally; forever	万花筒	wàn huā tǒng	kaleidoscope
万能	wàn néng	omnipotent	万家灯火	wàn jiā dēng huǒ	a myriad of twinkling lights

Example

万 一 有 人 找 我 ， 请 他 留 个 条 子 。
Wàn yī yǒu rén zhǎo wǒ,　qǐng tā liú gè tiáo·zi.

If by any chance somebody comes to see me, ask him to leave a message.

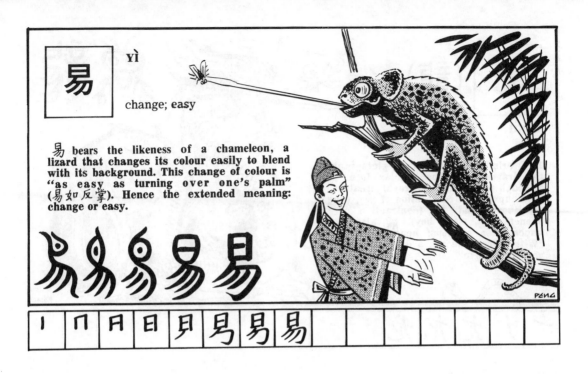

易　　YÌ

change; easy

易 bears the likeness of a chameleon, a lizard that changes its colour easily to blend with its background. This change of colour is "as easy as turning over one's palm" (易如反掌). Hence the extended meaning: change or easy.

易经	Yì Jīng	The Book of Changes
轻易	qīng yì	easily
容易	róng yì	easy
易燃物	yì rán wù	combustibles; inflammables
易如反掌	yì rú fǎn zhǎng	as easy as turning one's hand over — (fig.) very easy

Example

这 是 件 很 容 易 的 事 ， 让 我 来 做 吧 ！
Zhè shì jiàn hěn róng yì ·de shì, ràng wǒ lái zuò ·ba!
This is an easy matter, let me do it!

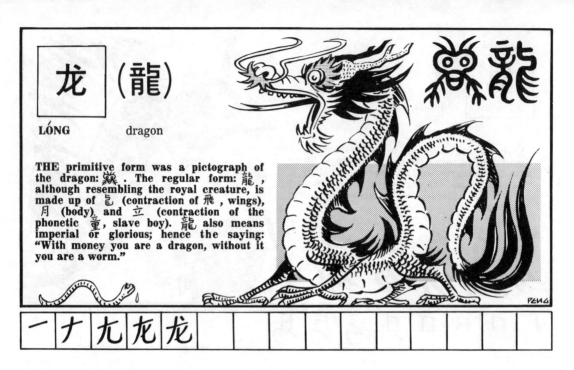

龙 (龍)

LÓNG   dragon

THE primitive form was a pictograph of the dragon: 龖 . The regular form: 龍 , although resembling the royal creature, is made up of 㔾 (contraction of 飛 , wings), 月 (body) and 立 (contraction of the phonetic 童 , slave boy). 龍 also means imperial or glorious; hence the saying: "With money you are a dragon, without it you are a worm."

一	十	尤	龙	龙

龙船	lóng chuán	dragon boat
龙卷	lóng juǎn	spout
龙虾	lóng xiā	lobster
龙眼	lóng yǎn	longan
龙钟	lóng zhōng	senile
龙卷风	lóng juǎn fēng	tornado
龙飞凤舞	lóng fēi fèng wǔ	like dragons flying and phoenixes dancing – (fig.) lively and vigorous
龙潭虎穴	lóng tán hǔ xuè	dragon's pool and tiger's den – (fig.) a danger spot
龙争虎斗	lóng zhēng hǔ dòu	a fierce struggle between two evenly-matched opponents

Example

龙 是 古 代 中 国 皇 族 的 象 征 。
Lóng shì gǔ dài Zhōng Guó huáng zú·de xiàng zhēng.
The dragon is a symbol of nobility in ancient China.

角 **JIĂO**

horn; corner;
10-cent piece

THE radical 角 resembles a
horn with its streaks. It is
probably a combination of
力 (strong) and 月 (flesh).
Because the horn terminates
in an angle and tapers to a
point, 角 can mean angle or
corner. 角 is also a 10-cent
piece, a mere tenth or "corner" of a dollar.

ノ　ク　ク　角　角　角　角

角尺	jiǎo chǐ	angle square	号角	hào jiǎo	bugle
角度	jiǎo dù	angle	鹿角	lù jiǎo	antler
角落	jiǎo luò	corner; nook	牛角	niú jiǎo	ox horn
角膜	jiǎo mó	cornea	角锥体	jiǎo zhuī tǐ	pyramid
角质	jiǎo zhì	cutin	角柱体	jiǎo zhù tǐ	prism

Example

在 院 子 的 一 个 角 落 里 有 一 棵 树 。
Zài yuàn‧zi‧de yī gè jiǎo luò‧li yǒu yī kē shù.

There is a tree in the corner of the courtyard.

JIĚ

divide; untie; explain

THIS character combines the radical for horn (角) with knife (刀) and ox (牛). To cleave the horn of an ox requires the use of a knife; hence 解: to divide. The horn of an ox is also shaped into bodkins (刀) for untying knots. So 解 also means to untie, undo, unravel and, by extension, explain. The ancient lexicon 说文解字 explains the origin of Chinese characters.

ノ ク ゲ 汐 夘 角 角 解 解 解 解 解 解

解除	jiě chú	remove	解闷	jiě mèn	divert oneself from boredom
解答	jiě dǎ	answer; explain	解剖	jiě pōu	dissect
解雇	jiě gù	discharge; dismiss	解脱	jiě tuō	free oneself
解决	jiě jué	solve; dispose of	溶解	róng jiě	dissolve
解开	jiě kāi	untie	注解	zhù jiě	explanatory notes

Example

我 们 终 于 解 决 了 这 个 难 题 。
Wǒ ·men zhōng yú jiě jué · le zhè gè nán tí.
We solved the problem finally.

毛 MÁO

hair; fur;
10-cent piece

毛 is a pictograph of the hair of man or beast. Compared with other parts of the body, the hair is insignificant and valueless. 毛 also means little, unpolished, or the common 10-cent piece. Our hairs may not be numbered but, says the proverb: "Pull a hair and the whole body may be affected."

毛笔	máo bǐ	writing brush
毛纺	máo fǎng	wool spinning
毛巾	máo jīn	towel
毛孔	máo kǒng	pore
毛毯	máo tǎn	woollen blanket

毛线	máo xiàn	knitting wool
毛衣	máo yī	woollen sweater
羽毛	yǔ máo	feather
毛毛雨	máo · mao yǔ	drizzle
毛骨悚然	máo gǔ sǒng rán	with one's hair standing on end — (fig.) absolutely terrified

Example

他 的 毛 病 是 性 急 。
Tā · de máo bìng shì xìng jí.

He is impetuous.

111

尾

WĚI

tail; end

尾 has 尸 (a recumbent body) as radical and 毛 (hair) as phonetic. In the seal form 毛 is inverted, indicating hair growing downwards from the body (尸), suggesting a tail: 尾. The tail is meant to be wagged by the body but when the people are strong and the ruler weak, "The tail is too large to wag" (尾大不掉).

フ　コ　尸　尸　尸　尾　尾

尾巴	wěi bā	tail
尾灯	wěi dēng	tail light; tail lamp
尾欠	wěi qiàn	balance due
尾声	wěi shēng	epilogue; end
尾随	wěi suí	tag along; follow at somebody's heel
尾追	wěi zhuī	in hot pursuit

Example

这 个 研 讨 会 已 接 近 尾 声 了 。
Zhè gè yán tǎo huì yǐ jiē jìn wěi shēng·le.

This seminar is drawing to an end.

老 LǍO

old; aged

THE seal character for "old" grew out of 𡿨 (hair), 人 (person) and 匕 (change). When the hair of man turns gray or white, its colour has changed, indicating old age: 耂, now arbitrarily shrunk to 老. To encourage respect for white hair, the old saying warns: "Laugh at the old, and age will laugh at you."

一 十 土 耂 耂 老

老板	lǎo bǎn	boss; employer	
老成	lǎo chéng	experienced; steady	
老将	lǎo jiàng	veteran; old-timer	
老练	lǎo liàn	seasoned; experienced	
老年	lǎo nián	old age	

老实	lǎo shí	honest; frank
老气横秋	lǎo qì héng qiū	lacking in youthful vigour
老生常谈	lǎo shēng cháng tán	common place; platitude
老羞成怒	lǎo xiū chéng nù	fly into a rage out of shame
老着脸皮	lǎo·zhe liǎn pí	unabashedly; unblushingly

Example

她 办 事 很 老练 。

Tā bàn shì hěn lǎo liàn.

She works with an experienced hand.

113

票 **PIÀO**

bill; ticket; ballot

THE early seal form:  represents an ancient method of signalling — fire (火) with rising smoke (彡) manipulated by four hands (彐彐). This suggests ticket or ballot, a form of sign. Another seal form: depicts the mischievous fairy of the phantom-fire, a dreaded natural phenomenon. It stands for bill or warrant — things also dreaded. The modern arbitrary form: 票 may be remembered as a bank bill, a western (西) token (示).

一 ㇀ ㇕ 币 西 西 西 覀 票 票 票

票额	piào'é	the sum stated on a cheque or bill; denomination	
票房	piào fáng	booking office	
票根	piào gēn	counterfoil; stub	
票价	piào jià	the price of a ticket	
票面	piào miàn	nominal value	

票箱	piào xiāng	ballot box
票子	piào · zi	bank note; paper money; bill
绑票	bǎng piào	kidnap
车票	chē piào	ticket (bus)
投票	tóu piào	vote

Example

这 场 戏 是 要 凭 票 入 场 的 。

Zhè chǎng xì shì yào píng piào rù chǎng · de.

Admission to this show is by ticket only.

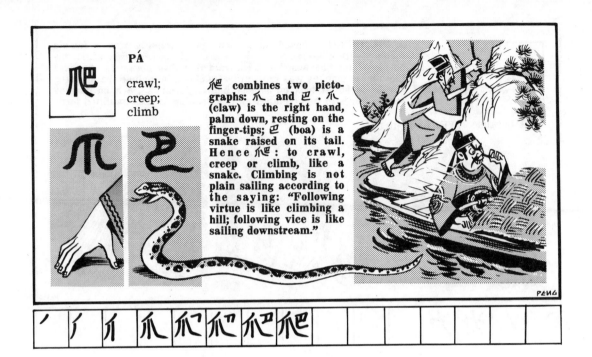

PÁ

crawl;
creep;
climb

爬 combines two pictographs: 爪 and 巴. 爪 (claw) is the right hand, palm down, resting on the finger-tips; 巴 (boa) is a snake raised on its tail. Hence 爬: to crawl, creep or climb, like a snake. Climbing is not plain sailing according to the saying: "Following virtue is like climbing a hill; following vice is like sailing downstream."

爬虫	pá chóng	reptile; insect
爬竿	pá gān	climbing pole; pole-climbing
爬犁	pá lí	sledge
爬山	pá shān	mountain-climbing
爬行	pá xíng	crawl; creep

Example

蛇 正 往 洞 里 爬 。

Shé zhèng wǎng dòng · li pá.

The snake is crawling into the hole.

115

为 (爲)

A PICTOGRAPH based on reason, 爲 originally was a female monkey with a human body: 爲 because of the resemblance. It was borrowed for "because" and contracted to two claws: 爲 because the female monkey was most prone to claw. To include the meaning "to do, to be" it took on a more human form: 爲, a hand carding textile fibres to remove unessentials, leading to the simplified form: 为

WÈI because   **WÉI** to be; to do

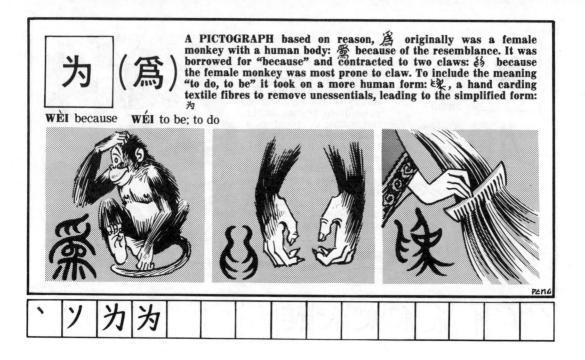

丶	ソ	为	为								

为何	wéi hé	why
为难	wéi nán	feel awkward; make things difficult
为期	wéi qī	by a definite date; duration
为人	wéi rén	behave; conduct oneself
为止	wéi zhǐ	up to

为重	wéi zhòng	attach most importance to
为主	wéi zhǔ	give priority to
为非作歹	wéi fēi zuò dǎi	do evil
为富不仁	wéi fù bù rén	be rich and cruel; be one of the heartless rich
为所欲为	wéi suǒ yù wéi	have one's own way

Example

他 是 新 来 的 同 事 ， 大 家 千 万 不 可 为 难 他 。

Tā shì xīn lái · de tóng shì, dà jiā qiān wàn bù kě wéi nán tā.

He's a new colleague, we should not make things difficult for him.

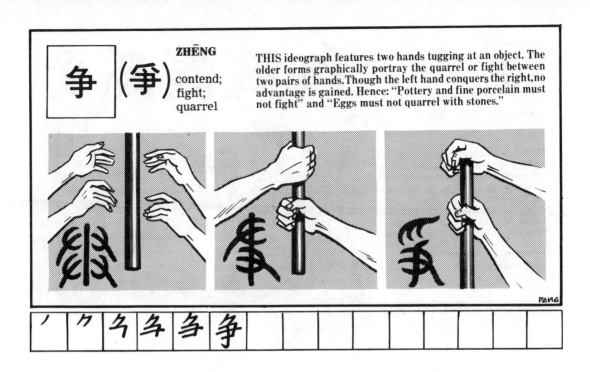

ZHĒNG

争 (爭) contend;
fight;
quarrel

THIS ideograph features two hands tugging at an object. The older forms graphically portray the quarrel or fight between two pairs of hands. Though the left hand conquers the right, no advantage is gained. Hence: "Pottery and fine porcelain must not fight" and "Eggs must not quarrel with stones."

争辩	zhēng biàn	argue
争吵	zhēng chǎo	quarrel
争持	zhēng chí	refuse to give in
争斗	zhēng dòu	fight; struggle; strife
争端	zhēng duān	controversial issue; dispute; conflict

争夺	zhēng duó	fight
争论	zhēng lùn	controversy; dispute
争执	zhēng zhí	disagree; dispute; argue
争权夺利	zhēng quán duó lì	scramble for power and profit
争先恐后	zhēng xiān kǒng hòu	strive to be the first and fear to lag behind

Example

你 们 在 争 论 什 么 ?

Nǐ·men zài zhēng lùn shěn·me?

What are all of you arguing about?

117

SHÒU

receive; accept

THIS character represents the loading of goods. A hand (⼑), on the bank, delivers the goods while another hand (又), in the boat, (舟) receives and stows them away in the hold. In the seal forms the boat can be seen in symbol: 夕, eventually contracted to ⼂ and ∩. The ideograph, by extension, means "receive, accept, endure."

受苦	shòu kǔ	suffer	受气	shòu qì	be bullied
受难	shòu nàn	suffer calamities	受伤	shòu shāng	be wounded
受罚	shòu fá	be punished	受益	shòu yì	benefit from
受害	shòu hài	victimised	享受	xiǎng shòu	enjoy
受惊	shòu jīng	be frightened; be startled	受不了	shòu bù liǎo	cannot bear; unable to endure

Example

他 受 不 了 老 板 的 态 度 。

Tā shòu bù liǎo lǎo bǎn·de tài dù.

He cannot tolerate the boss's attitude.

118

GǓ

bone

The bones form the framework of the body and are closely associated with the flesh. The character for bone: 骨 therefore combines pictographs of the bone (咼) and flesh (肉). However, courtesy demands that you ask for a bone if you want flesh, despite the saying: "You can't get fat from a dry bone."

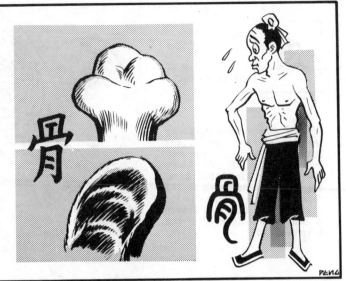

| | | | | | | | | | | | | |
|丶|冂|冂|冎|冎|咼|咼|骨|骨|骨| | | |

骨骼	gǔ gé	skeleton	骨气	gǔ qì	moral integrity
骨灰	gǔ huī	ashes of the dead	骨肉	gǔ ròu	flesh and blood
骨架	gǔ jià	framework	骨折	gǔ zhé	fracture
骨节	gǔ jié	joint	骨子里	gǔ·zi lǐ	in one's heart of hearts
骨牌	gǔ pái	dominoes	骨瘦如柴	gǔ shòu rú chái	a bag of bones

Example

他 是 一 个 有 骨 气 的 人 。
Tā shì yī gè yǒu gǔ qì ·de rén.

He is a man of integrity.

皮

PÍ

skin; leather

THREE components make up the character for skin: 又, the hand that flays; ノ, the animal skin; and 刀, the knife. The animal skin, being durable, may be compared to the reputation of a man, as in the saying: "Man dies and leaves a name; the tiger dies and leaves a skin."

フ	厂	广	皮	皮								

皮袄	pí ˙ǎo	fur-lined jacket
皮包	pí bāo	leather handbag
皮带	pí dài	leather belt
皮蛋	pí dàn	preserved egg
皮肤	pí fū	skin
皮箱	pí xiāng	leather suitcase
皮鞋	pí xié	leather shoes
皮鞭子	pí biān ˙zi	leather-thonged whip

Example

他　踏　到　香　蕉　皮　，　摔　了　一　跤　。
Tā　tà　dào　xiāng jiāo　pí,　shuāi˙le　yī　jiāo.

He stepped on a banana skin and slipped.

120

假 JIǍ false

IN THE seal form, 二 (two) added to 叚 (skin) produces 叚, two skins or double skin — a borrowed skin over one's true skin — suggesting a disguise, a falsehood. Clarified by the radical for man (亻), the character has special application to man, the one most guilty of falsehood: 假. Truth exaggerated becomes a falsehood, and when "one man tells a falsehood, a hundred repeat it as truth."

丿	亻	仃	仃	伩	伩	作	作	假	假	假		

假扮	jiǎ bàn	disguise oneself
假充	jiǎ chōng	pretend to be
假定	jiǎ dìng	suppose
假想	jiǎ xiǎng	imagination
假如	jiǎ rú	if

假设	jiǎ shè	suppose
假面具	jiǎ miàn jù	mask; false front
假惺惺	jiǎ xīng·xing	hypocritically; unctuously
假公济私	jiǎ gōng jì sī	use public office for private gain
假仁假义	jiǎ rén jiǎ yì	hypocrisy

Example

假 如 我 忘 了 ， 请 提 醒 我 一 下 。
Jiǎ rú wǒ wàng·le, qǐng tí xǐng wǒ yī xià.

Please remind me if I forget.

121

须 (須)

XŪ must; wait; beard

THIS is a pictograph showing a man's head (百) upon his body (儿) with hair (彡) on his face — his beard: 须 .

In ancient days, it was necessary for a man to wait for the right time to grow a beard, namely, when he was master of a family. Hence the extended meanings: must, necessary, wait.

丿 夂 彡 彡 纟 纟 须 须 须

须要	xū yào	have to
须知	xū zhī	one should know that
须发	xū fà	beard and hair
须根	xū gēn	fibrous root
须臾	xū yú	moment; instant
必须	bì xū	must
留须	liú xū	grow a beard

Example

做 这 项 工 作 须 要 细 心 。
Zuò zhè xiàng gōng zuò xū yào xì xīn.

This work needs to be done with care.

头 (頭)

TÓU head

頭 has 頁 for radical and 豆 for phonetic. 頁 is a picture of a head (首) upon the body (儿). 豆 is a sacrificial vessel for serving meat; it suggests the skull, containing the meaty part of the body, the brain. Hence 頭 the head, where the brain is contained. The simplified form may have lost its head: 头 , but the saying still goes: "You can cut off the head but you can't stop the tongue."

头版	tóu bǎn	front page (of a newspaper)
头等	tóu děng	first-class
头发	tóu fà	hair
头昏	tóu hūn	dizzy; giddy
头巾	tóu jīn	scarf
头脑	tóu nǎo	brains; mind
头疼	tóu téng	headache
头头是道	tóu tóu shì dào	closely reasoned and well argued
茫无头绪	máng wú tóu xù	be in a hopeless tangle

Example

她 很 有 头 脑 。
Tā hěn yǒu tóu nǎo.
She has a good brain.

123

虫 （蟲）

CHÓNG   insect; worm

THE seal form of the radical 虫 represents a snake or worm. 蟲, the triple-form, includes small crawling, creeping or swarming creatures like bugs, insects, worms and reptiles (now simplified to 虫). Hinting at the predatory habits of human beings, the saying goes: "While the mantis is after the cicada, the sparrow is not far behind."

丶	冂	口	中	虫	虫						

虫灾	chóng zāi	plague of insects
虫子	chóng · zi	insect; worm
害虫	hài chóng	destructive insect (pest)
蛔虫	huí chóng	roundworm
益虫	yì chóng	(beneficial) insect
幼虫	yòu chóng	larva
寄生虫	jì shēng chóng	parasite
微生虫	wēi shēng chóng	bacteria

Example

蛔 虫 是 肚 子 里 的 寄 生 虫 。
Huí chóng shì dù · zi lǐ · de jì shēng chóng.

Roundworms are parasites in the stomach.

蚁（蟻）

YǏ ant

蚁, the character for ant, has 虫 (insect) for radical and 义 (righteous) for phonetic. Being social insects living in organised colonies, ants appear civilised or "righteous". Like human-beings, they have a government, an army and a communication system; they harvest and even keep "slaves" and "cows". Also, like human beings inclined to evil and vice, "Swarms of ants cling on to the rotten carcass." (群蚁附膻)

丶 冂 口 中 虫 虫 虫ˋ 虫ノ 蚁

蚁蚕	yǐ cán	newly-hatched silkworm
蚁巢	yǐ cháo	ant nest
蚁丘	yǐ qiū	ant hill
蚂蚁	mǎ yǐ	ant

Example

蚂 蚁 可 以 扛 起 比 自 己 大 几 倍 的 东 西 。

Mǎ yǐ kě yǐ gāng qǐ bǐ zì jǐ dà jǐ bèi · de dōng · xi.

An ant can carry a load several times its size.

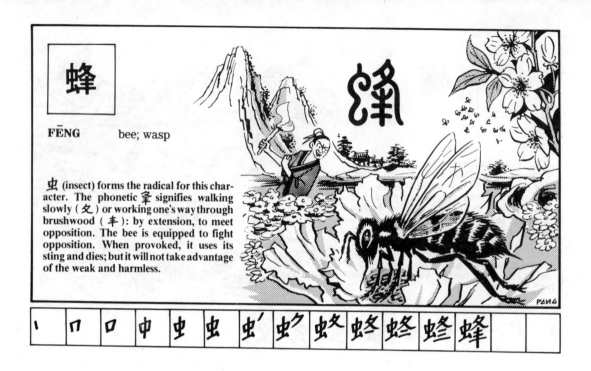

蜂

FĒNG bee; wasp

虫 (insect) forms the radical for this character. The phonetic 夆 signifies walking slowly (夂) or working one's way through brushwood (丰): by extension, to meet opposition. The bee is equipped to fight opposition. When provoked, it uses its sting and dies; but it will not take advantage of the weak and harmless.

丶 丨 冂 口 中 虫 虫 虫′ 虫夂 蚁 蛴 蜂 蜂 蜂

蜂巢	fēng cháo	honeycomb	蜂鸟	fēng niǎo	hummingbird
蜂刺	fēng cì	the sting of a bee or wasp	蜂乳	fēng rǔ	royal jelly
蜂毒	fēng dú	bee venom	蜂王	fēng wáng	queen bee; queen wasp
蜂蜡	fēng là	beeswax	蜂拥	fēng yōng	swarm; flock
蜂蜜	fēng mì	honey	蜜蜂	mì fēng	honeybee

Example

蜂 蜜 营 养 丰 富 。

Fēng mì yíng yǎng fēng fù.

Honey is nutritious.

126

DIÉ

蝶

butterfly

THE character for butterfly: 蝶, the most beautiful of insects, is based on the radical 虫 (insect). It owes its beauty to its colourful leaf-like wings, some species even mimicking leaves. Fittingly, its phonetic: 枼 is a representation of leaves that reappear yearly — the successive generations (世) of a tree (木).

蝶骨	dié gǔ	sphenoid bone
蝶泳	dié yǒng	butterfly stroke (swimming)
蝴蝶	hú dié	butterfly

Example

蝴 蝶 在 花 间 嬉 戏 。

Hú dié zài huā jiān xī xì.

Butterflies are playing among the flowers.

虾（蝦）

XIĀ   prawn; shrimp

蝦 the shrimp, sheds its skin while growing another. It is the creature with a false (叚) skin, literally two (二) skins (皮). 蝦 is now simplified to 虾 — the creature (虫) below (下) or low-down. Combining the puny shrimp with the mighty dragon produces the lobster (龙虾). But comparing them generates the proverb: "The dragon in shallow water becomes the butt of shrimps."

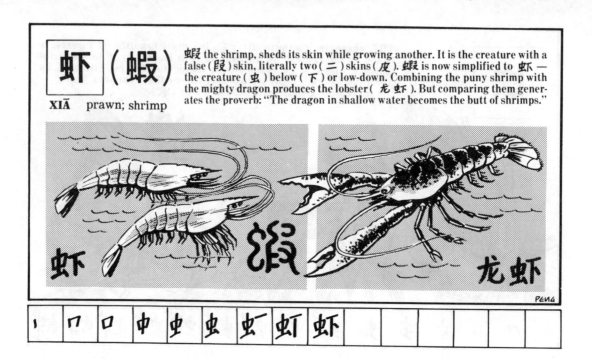

丶 丨 口 口 中 虫 虫 虫 虾 虾

虾饼	xiā bǐng	prawn-crackers	
虾干	xiā gān	dried shrimps	
虾蛄	xiā gū	mantis shrimp	
虾酱	xiā jiàng	shrimp paste	
虾米	xiā mǐ	dried, shelled shrimps	
虾皮	xiā pí	dried small shrimps	

虾群	xiā qún	a shoal of shrimps
虾仁	xiā rén	shelled fresh shrimps; shrimp meat
龙虾	lóng xiā	lobster
虾兵蟹将	xiā bīng xiè jiàng	shrimp soldiers and crab generals — ineffective troops

Example

我 弟 弟 喜 欢 吃 虾 饼 。
Wǒ dì·di xǐ huān chī xiā bǐng.

My brother likes prawn-crackers.

蛇

SHÉ snake; serpent

蛇 features 虫 (reptile) as radical and 它 (snake) as phonetic. 它 is probably a cobra, poised on its tail (∪), with distended neck (宀) and darting tongue (ノ). Snakes prey on lizards, mice, birds and even larger creatures, swallowing them whole. Hence the saying: "A man whose heart is not content is like a snake which tries to swallow an elephant."

`ヽ 冂 口 中 虫 虫 虫' 虫' 虫' 虫' 蛇`

蟒蛇	mǎng shé	python
水蛇	shuǐ shé	water snake
四脚蛇	sì jiǎo shé	lizard
响尾蛇	xiǎng wěi shé	rattlesnake
眼镜蛇	yǎn jìng shé	cobra
杯弓蛇影	bēi gōng shé yǐng	mistaking the reflection of a bow in the cup for a snake — extremely suspicious

Example

蟒 蛇 是 无 毒 的 。
Mǎng shé shì wú dú · de
Pythons have no venom.

129

蛋

DÀN egg

蛋 refers to the ball rolled (疋) by the dung-beetle (虫) for food or for breeding; by extension, egg. 疋 (seal form of 疋) signifies the foot (止) turning or rolling (ᓂ). Paired beetles work closely together to mould, roll and bury the dung-ball housing the egg. With poultry, however, the cock crows, but the hen lays the egg.

蛋白	dàn bái	egg-white
蛋粉	dàn fěn	powdered eggs
蛋糕	dàn gāo	cake
蛋黄	dàn huáng	yolk
蛋壳	dàn ké	egg-shell
蛋品	dàn pǐn	egg products
蛋清	dàn qīng	egg-white

蛋白质	dàn bái zhì	protein
蛋用鸡	dàn yòng jī	layer
鸡飞蛋打	jī fēi dàn dǎ	the hen has flown away and the eggs in the coop are broken — all is lost

Example

多 吃 含 有 蛋 白 质 的 东 西 对 身 体 有 益 。
Duō chī hán yǒu dàn bái zhì ·de dōng ·xi duì shēn tǐ yǒu yì.

More protein is good for the body.

风 (風)

FĒNG   wind

THE seal form: 鳳 is based on man's belief that insects (虫) are born under the influence of the wind or vapour (凡). An older form: 颩 — from 日 (sun), ノ (motion) and 凡 (extension) — suggests that wind is produced by the action of the sun. The simplified form, however, cuts out the sun and insects, leaving the motion and extension; 风, which goes to prove that "Man's words are like grass — they sway with the wind."

ノ	几	凡	风							

风采	fēng cǎi	elegant demeanour
风干	fēng gān	air-dry
风格	fēng gé	style
风光	fēng guāng	scene; view
风浪	fēng làng	stormy waves; storm

风靡	fēng mǐ	fashionable
风气	fēng qì	general mood; atmosphere
风趣	fēng qù	humour; wit
风俗	fēng sú	custom
风云人物	fēng yún rén wù	man of the hour

Example

迷 你 裙 曾 经 风 靡 一 时 。

Mí nǐ qún céng jīn fēng mǐ yī shí.

The mini-skirt was all the rage at one time.

131

GŌNG

公

public;
impartial

公 is made up of 八 (division, opposition) and 厶 (private, selfish), a pictograph of a silkworm coiled in its cocoon. It implies the division (八) of private (厶) property for the benefit of the public. Hence 公, meaning public or impartial, i.e., opposed (八) to private or selfish (厶).

ノ	八	公	公									

公道　gōng dào　reasonable
公共　gōng gòng　public
公分　gōng fēn　centimetre (cm)
公愤　gōng fèn　public indignation;
　　　　　　　　popular anger
公民　gōng mín　citizen
公式　gōng shì　formula

公司　gōng sī　company; corporation
公用　gōng yòng　for public use
公寓　gōng yù　apartment
公园　gōng yuán　park
公制　gōng zhì　the metric system
公众　gōng zhòng　the public

Example

这 个 电 话 是 公 用 的 。
Zhè · ge diàn huà shì gōng yòng · de.
This telephone is for public use.

SĪ

私

personal;
private;
selfish

THE radical 禾 stands for grain, man's staple food, a highly valued possession. The phonetic ム , representing a silkworm hidden in its cocoon, symbolises private or selfish. Grain (禾) in ancient days was used to pay taxes and the residue was personal (ム) property. Hence 私 : my share of grain, i.e., personal, private or selfish.

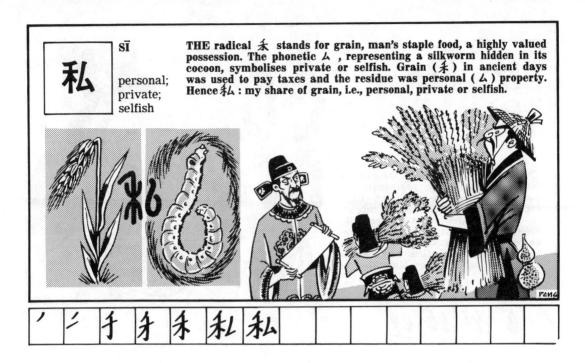

丿 二 千 牙 禾 私 私

私奔	sī bēn	elopement
私立	sī lì	privately run
私人	sī rén	private
私事	sī shì	private (or personal) affairs
私语	sī yǔ	whisper

无私	wú sī	selfless
自私	zì sī	selfish
私生活	sī shēng huó	private life
私生子	sī shēng zǐ	illegitimate child
大公无私	dà gōng wú sī	selfless; unselfish

Example

自 私 的 行 为 是 要 不 得 的 。
zì sī · de xíng wéi shì yào bù dé · de.

Selfish acts are undesirable.

丝 （絲）

SĪ　silk

替 is the seal form of 糸, the radical for silk. The upper 呂 represents two cocoons; the lower part 小, the twisting of several strands into a thread. 糸 is duplicated to stand for silk, indicating that many threads are required to form silk: 絲. In the modern version the two identical components are woven together and simplified to 丝.

㇜	纟	纟纟	纟纟	纟纟					

丝绸	sī chóu	silk cloth		丝织品	sī zhī pǐn	silk fabrics
丝带	sī dài	silk ribbon; silk braid; silk sash		丝丝入扣	sī sī rù kòu	(done) with meticulous care and flawless artistry
丝毫	sī háo	a bit		一丝不挂	yī sī bù guà	not have a stitch on; be stark-naked
丝绒	sī róng	velvet				
丝状	sī zhuàng	filiform		一丝一毫	yī sī yī háo	a tiny bit; an iota; a trace
肉丝	ròu sī	meat floss				

Example

她 脸 上 没 有 一 丝 笑 容 。
Tā liǎn shàng méi yǒu yī sī xiào róng.

There isn't a trace of a smile on her face.

XIÀN thread

THE radical is 糸 (silk). The phonetic 戔 means small, fine or split into bits — the common work of many spears (戈). Hence 綫: thread, made up of minute (戔) strands of silk (糸). Another version is 線, with 泉 (spring) as phonetic. Here the thread is likened to a continuous flow of water from a spring. Whichever the version, "The thread cannot pass without a needle; the boat cannot cross without water."

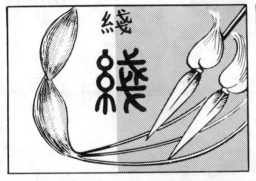 

线虫   xiàn chóng   nematode
线段   xiàn duàn   line segment
线描   xiàn miáo   line drawing
线绳   xiàn shéng   cotton rope
线索   xiàn suǒ   clue

线装   xiàn zhuāng   traditional thread binding (of Chinese books)
光线   guāng xiàn   light ray
铜线   tóng xiàn   copper wire
直线   zhí xiàn   straight line
线轴儿   xiàn zhóur   bobbin

Example

那 些 难 民 在 饥 饿 线 上 挣 扎 。
Nà xiē nàn mín zài jī è xiàn shàng zhēng zhá.

The refugees are struggling against starvation.

红（紅）

HÓNG red

RED is a happy, auspicious colour, most pleasing to the Chinese. Because it is not the natural colour of silk (糸), extra work (工) has to be put in to dye it red: 红. Red, however, is not always propitious, as in the saying: 红颜薄命 (Beautiful women are often unfortunate).

红豆	hóng dòu	red beans; red seeds	红运	hóng yùn	good luck
红海	Hóng Hǎi	Red Sea	红肿	hóng zhǒng	red and swollen
红利	hóng lì	bonus	口红	kǒu hóng	lipstick
红润	hóng rùn	rosy	红白事	hóng bái shì	weddings and funerals
红晕	hóng yùn	blush; flush	红绿灯	hóng lǜ dēng	traffic lights; traffic signals

Example

他 的 脸 上 泛 出 红 晕 。
Tā · de liǎn shàng fàn chū · hóng yùn.

His face was red.

给（給）

GEǏ   give; provide; supply

GIFTS foster unity and harmony (合) between friends and relatives; and what better present than silk (系), a material appreciated by all. Hence 給, meaning to give and, by extension, to provide or supply. The practice of giving brings blessings, for there is more happiness in giving than there is in receiving.

⺀	乞	纟	纟	纩	纶	纶	给	给				

给以   gěi yǐ   give; grant

Example

这 本 书 是 给 你 的 。
Zhè běn shū ·shì gěi nǐ · de.

This book is for you.

结 (結)

JIÉ

knot;
produce;
settle

THE phonetic 吉 means fortunate — from 士 (affair) and 口 (mouth) — an affair worth announcing. In this character, the radical 糸 (silk) enforces the idea of tying or making secure something fortunate, e.g., concluding a contract, producing fruitage or tying a knot: 結. Illustrated is the successful conclusion of an affair worth announcing — the tying of the matrimonial knot.

结婚

ㄥ　纟　纟　纟　纟　纟　纟　结　结

结拜	jié bài	become sworn brothers or sisters
结冰	jié bīng	freeze
结彩	jié cǎi	adorn or decorate
结果	jié guǒ	result; outcome
结合	jié hé	combine

结婚	jié hūn	get married
结论	jié lùn	conclusion
结盟	jié méng	form an alliance
结清	jié qīng	settle
结束	jié shù	end

Example

油 漆 上 面 结 了 一 层 皮 。

Yóu qī shàng miàn jié · le yī céng pí.

A layer of skin formed on the paint.

纸 (紙)

ZHǏ paper

THE phonetic 氏 (clan) was originally a floating plant (屮) spread out flat (⼁) over the water surface, rooting itself to the bottom. Silk (糸) — the radical — is also spread out when used as a writing material. Hence 纸: paper — the writing material like silk (糸) that lies flat and apparently harmless as the water-plant (氏). But beware: "Paper and brush may kill a man; you don't need a knife."

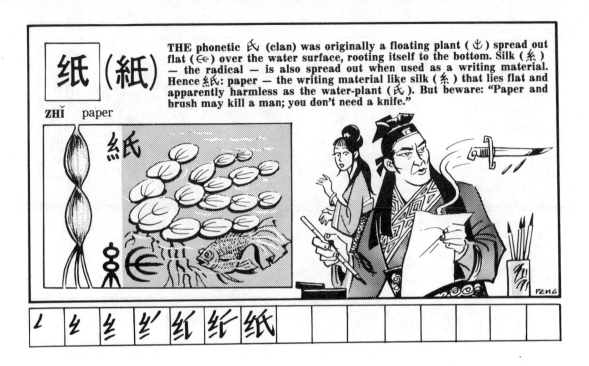

纸板	zhǐ bǎn	paperboard; cardboard
纸币	zhǐ bì	paper money; currency note
纸盒	zhǐ hé	box; carton
纸花	zhǐ huā	paper flower
纸牌	zhǐ pái	playing cards

纸型	zhǐ xíng	paper mould
纸鸢	zhǐ yuān	kite
纸张	zhǐ zhāng	paper
报纸	bào zhǐ	newspaper
纸上谈兵	zhǐ shàng tán bīng	be an armchair strategist

Example

这 朵 纸 花 很 美 。
Zhè duǒ zhǐ huā hěn měi.

This paper flower is very pretty.

网 （網）

WǍNG　net

THIS character started as a pictograph of a net: 网. It was cast aside and replaced by the regular form 網, comprising 糸 (silk) and 罔 (trap) — without much success. So the primitive pictograph of the net was taken up again for the modern simplified form 网, demonstrating that: "There is a day to cast your nets, and a day to dry your nets."

丶　冂　冈　网　网　网

网罗	wǎng luó	trap
网球	wǎng qiú	tennis
电网	diàn wǎng	electrified barbed wire
发网	fà wǎng	hair net
漏网	lòu wǎng	slip through the net; escape unpunished
鱼网	yú wǎng	fish net

广播网	guǎng bō wǎng	broadcasting network
蜘蛛网	zhī zhū wǎng	cobweb
天罗地网	tiān luó dì wǎng	nets above and snares below — tight encirclement
网开一面	wǎng kāi yī miàn	leave one side of the net open — give the wrongdoer a way out

Example

这 个 鱼 网 破 了 。

Zhè·ge　yú wǎng　pò·le.

This fish net is torn.

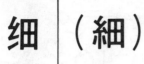

XÌ fine; tender; careful

IN THIS character, the phonetic 田 was originally written: ⊗ , a top view of the child's skull showing the tender fontanelles. Hence 細, meaning tender, fine, soft, like the silken (糸) hair around the fontanelles (⊗). Small beginnings are not to be despised for, just as resources last a long time if used sparingly, "A small stream flows without interruption."

⺡	幺	幺	纟	纫	织	细	细					

细胞	xì bāo	cell	细密	xì mì	fine and closely woven
细长	xì cháng	tall and slender	细腻	xì nì	exquisite
细工	xì gōng	fine workmanship	细心	xì xīn	careful; attentive
细节	xì jié	minute detail	细小	xì xiǎo	very small; tiny
细菌	xì jūn	germ	仔细	zǐ xì	careful; attentive

Example

她 做 事 很 细 心 。
Tā zuò shì hěn xì xīn.

She is very careful in everything she does.

经 （經）

JĪNG　classic; already; pass through

THE phonetic 坙 was originally 壬 — an allusion to water currents (巛) under the ground (一) that the geomancer examines (壬) — something deep, not superficial. In the regular form, the phonetic resembles warp threads on a loom: 坙. Just as silk threads (糸) are woven into precious fabrics, so wisdom is woven into enduring classics: 經, a literary heritage that has already passed through many hands.

| 乚 | 乡 | 纟 | 纟フ | 经 | 纾 | 经 | | | | | | |

经常	jīng cháng	frequently	经过	jīng guò	pass through; pass by
经典	jīng diǎn	classics	经济	jīng jì	economy
经度	jīng dù	longitude	经纪	jīng jì	broker; manage (a business)
经费	jīng fèi	funds	经理	jīng lǐ	manager; manage
经管	jīng guǎn	be in charge of	经传	jīng zhuàn	classics

Example

这 车 经 过 动 物 园 吗 ？
Zhè chē jīng guò dòng wù yuán‧ma?

Does this car pass by the zoo?

终（終）

ZHŌNG　end; final

THIS character has 冬 (winter) for its phonetic. Its seal form was a bundle of silk tied at the end by a band to suggest "end": 𣂭 . Ice (冫) was added to signify winter, the end of the year. The presence of the silk radical (糸) extends the idea to "the winter of the silk thread," i.e., the final part of it, the end: 终.

终场	zhōng chǎng	end of a performance or show	终年	zhōng nián	throughout the year
终点	zhōng diǎn	destination; finishing line	终身	zhōng shēn	lifelong
终古	zhōng gǔ	forever	终于	zhōng yú	finally
终归	zhōng guī	eventually; after all	终止	zhōng zhǐ	stop; terminate
终究	zhōng jiū	eventually; in the end	临终	lín zhōng	on one's death-bed

Example

一 个 人 的 力 量 终 究 有 限 。
Yí · ge rén · de lì liàng zhōng jiū yǒu xiàn.
The strength of an individual is limited after all.

143

维 （維）

WÉI   tie; fasten; safeguard

维 is an ideograph composed of two pictographs: 糸 (silk) and 隹 (bird). It represents a silk thread attached to a bird, suggesting to tie, fasten or secure, hence to safeguard or maintain. Often used in a good sense, 维 is incorporated in transliterations of words like vitamin, Venus, Victoria, Virginia, etc.

乚 纟 纟 纟 纠 纤 纤 绊 维 维 维

维持	wéi chí	maintain; keep
维护	wéi hù	safeguard
维系	wéi xì	hold together; maintain
维新	wéi xīn	reform
维修	wéi xiū	service; maintain
思维	sī wéi	thought; thinking
维他命	wéi tā mìng	vitamin
维妙维肖	wéi miào wéi xiào	remarkably true to life; absolutely lifelike

Example

大 家 需 要 互 相 了 解 ， 才 能 维 持 友 好 关 系 。
Dà jiā xū yào hù xiāng liáo jiě, cái néng wéi chí yǒu hǎo guān xì.

To maintain our friendly relations, we need to understand one another.

144

罗（羅）

羅 is a sieve or net (罒 or 罓) of silk (糸) for catching birds (隹). It is usually round and flat. The simplified form reduces it to 罗, made up of 罒 (net) and 夕 (evening, slanting). Because the net resembles a gong, the addition of the metal radical 金 transforms it into the character for gong: 锣.

LUÓ   net for birds; sieve

丶	冖	冂	罒	罒	罗	罗	罗					

罗列	luó liè	spread out; set out; enumerate
罗马	Luó Mǎ	Rome
罗盘	luó pán	compass
罗网	luó wǎng	net; trap
罗织	luó zhī	frame-up
罗致	luó zhì	collect; enlist the services of
罗望子	luó wàng zǐ	tamarind
门可罗雀	mén kě luó què	catch sparrows on the doorstep — (fig.) visitors are few and far between
自投罗网	zì tóu luó wǎng	walk right into the trap

Example

他 到 处 罗 致 人 材 。
Tā dào chù luó zhì rén cái.

He went round enlisting the services of able people.

乐 （樂）

YUÈ music;
LÈ joy; pleasure

THE symbol for music was once five drums (⊗⊗⊗) - representing the five tones of the Chinese musical scale - upon a stand of wood (木). The regular form 樂 is now simplified to 乐, shaped after the music stand. The symbol for music 樂, pronounced differently, means joy or pleasure, for music gladdens the heart of man.

丿 ㇄ 乒 乐 乐

乐队	yuè duì	orchestra; band	
乐谱	yuè pǔ	music score	
乐器	yuè qì	musical instrument	
声乐	shēng yuè	vocal music	
音乐	yīn yuè	music	

乐观	lè guān	optimistic
乐趣	lè qù	delight
乐意	lè yì	pleased; happy
乐不可支	lè bù kě zhī	overjoyed
乐极生悲	lè jí shēng bēi	extreme joy begets sorrow

Example

他 对 前 途 感 到 乐 观 。
Tā duì qián tú gǎn dào lè guān.
He is optimistic about his future.

146

药 (藥)

YÀO medicine

MEDICINAL herbs (艹), like music that soothes the mind, restore harmony (樂) to the body; hence 樂 , the symbol for medicine. The simplified form 药 combines 艹 (herbs) with 约 (agree, restrain), implying that herbs restrain sickness. Though there are herbal remedies for all sorts of ailments: "No medicine can cure a man of vulgarity."

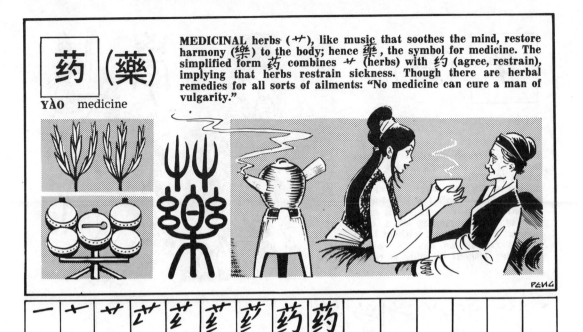

一 十 艹 艹 艹 艻 茓 药 药 药

药草	yào cǎo	medicinal herbs
药方	yào fāng	prescription
药房	yào fáng	dispensary
药水	yào shuǐ	lotion; liquid medicine
药丸	yào wán	pill
服药	fú yào	take medicine
火药	huǒ yào	gunpowder
杀虫药	shā chóng yào	insecticide

Example

这 药 很 苦 。
Zhè yào hěn kǔ.

This medicine is bitter.

学 （學）

XUÉ   learn; study

THIS ideograph signifies enlightenment — the master's laying on of hands (⼹⺕) crosswise (乂) upon the darkness which covers (冖) the mind of his disciple (子). It implies to learn or study. Learning is essential to the upbringing of a child, hence: "To raise a son without learning is raising an ass; to raise a daughter without learning is raising a pig."

PENG

丶　丷　丷　丷　ⱽ　学　学

学费	xué fèi	tuition fee
学府	xué fǔ	an institution of learning
学科	xué kē	branch of learning; subject
学生	xué shēng	student; pupil
学识	xué shí	knowledge
学徒	xué tú	apprentice; trainee
学校	xué xiào	school
学无止境	xué wú zhǐ jìng	knowledge is infinite
学以致用	xué yǐ zhì yòng	study for the purpose of application

Example

你 的 功 课 学 会 了 吗 ?
Nǐ · de gōng kè xué hùi · le · ma?

Have you learned your lessons?

写 (寫)

XIĚ write

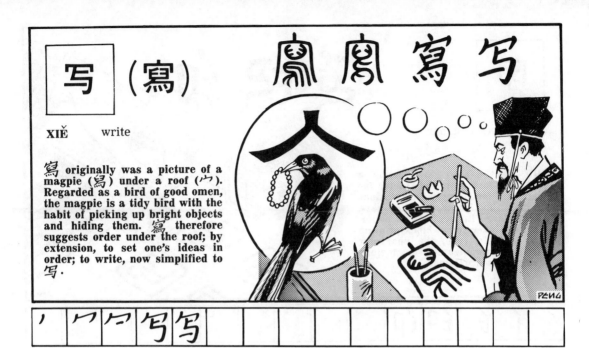

寫 originally was a picture of a magpie (舄) under a roof (宀). Regarded as a bird of good omen, the magpie is a tidy bird with the habit of picking up bright objects and hiding them. 寫 therefore suggests order under the roof; by extension, to set one's ideas in order; to write, now simplified to 写.

写实	xiě shí	write or paint realistically
写稿	xiě gǎo	write for (a magazine, etc.)
写生	xiě shēng	draw, paint or sketch from nature
写照	xiě zhào	portrayal; portraiture
写作	xiě zuò	writing
写字台	xiě zì tái	writing desk

Example

他 经 常 为 报 章 ， 杂 志 写 稿 。
Tā jīng cháng wèi bào zhāng, zá zhì xiě gǎo.

He often writes for the newspapers and magazines.

149

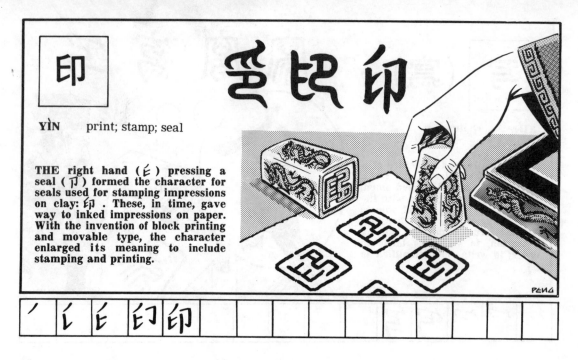

印

YÌN   print; stamp; seal

THE right hand (𤓰) pressing a
seal (卩) formed the character for
seals used for stamping impressions
on clay: 印 . These, in time, gave
way to inked impressions on paper.
With the invention of block printing
and movable type, the character
enlarged its meaning to include
stamping and printing.

PENG

´　𠂉　𣎳　印　印

印发	yìn fā	print and distribute
印盒	yìn hé	seal box
印花	yìn huā	revenue stamp
印刷	yìn shuā	printing
印台	yìn tái	ink pad; stamp pad
印象	yìn xiàng	impression
印章	yìn zhāng	seal
盖印	gài yìn	affix one's seal
印刷机	yìn shuā jī	printing machine

Example

这 照 片 印 得 不 清 楚 。
Zhè zhào piàn yìn · de bù qīng chǔ.

This photo is not well-printed

150

书 (書)

SHŪ book; writings

書 is the product of a pen (聿) that speaks (曰) — books and writings. 聿 indicates a stylus (丨) in hand (⺕) scratching a line (一) on a tablet (一). 曰, the radical, is the mouth (口) with a word (一) in it. Because not everything the pen speaks is truth, "It is better to have no books than to rely blindly on them."

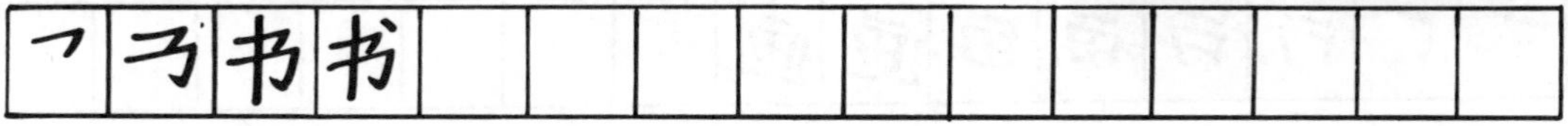

书包	shū bāo	schoolbag	书房	shū fáng	study room
书报	shū bào	books and newspapers	书籍	shū jí	books
书本	shū běn	book	书评	shū píng	book review
书店	shū diàn	bookshop	书生	shū shēng	scholar
书法	shū fǎ	calligraphy	书呆子	shū dāi · zi	bookworm

Example

这 是 一 间 小 书 店 ， 卖 的 书 不 多 。
Zhè shì yī jiān xiǎo shū diàn, mài · de shū bù duō.
This is a small bookshop. There aren't many books.

画 (畫)

HUÀ painting; drawing

畫, a painting or drawing, is symbolised by the artist's brush (聿) and his picture (田); of the frame there now remains only the bottom part (一). However, the simplified form: 画 restores the picture (田) with its frame (凵). "Painting a snake and adding legs" (画蛇添足) would be superfluous. Hence the need to be practical: "You cannot satisfy your hunger by merely drawing a loaf."

一 厂 厂 冎 币 币 画 画

画报	huà bào	pictorial
画家	huà jiā	painter; artist
画架	huà jià	easel
画廊	huà láng	gallery
画室	huà shì	studio
画象	huà xiàng	portrait
画展	huà zhǎn	art exhibition
画饼充饥	huà bǐng chōng jí	draw cakes to allay one's hunger — (fig.) feed on illusions
画蛇添足	huà shé tiān zú	draw a snake and add feet to it — (fig.) ruin the effect by adding something superfluous

Example

这 个 画 家 是 我 的 朋 友 。
Zhè · ge huà jiā shì wǒ · de péng yǒu.

This artist is my friend.

事 SHÌ

affair;
business;
matter

AN affair is a matter to be viewed seriously and executed faithfully. It is represented by two hands 十 and ヨ (contractions of 手) acting with fidelity 口 (contraction of 中): 事. Another view is that an affair is a business to be recorded accurately, symbolised by a hand (ヨ) with stylus (十) recording what is told by word of mouth (口): 事.

一　丁　冖　口　写　写　写　事

事故	shì gù	mishap
事后	shì hòu	after the event; afterwards
事迹	shì jī	deed
事件	shì jiàn	incident
事理	shì lǐ	reason; logic
事情	shì qíng	affair; matter
事实	shì shí	fact
事业	shì yè	undertaking; enterprise
事物	shì wù	thing
事倍功半	shì bèi gōng bàn	get half the result with twice the effort

Example

事　情　的　真　相　不　是　这　么　简　单　的 。
Shì　qíng · de　zhēn　xiàng　bú　shì　zhè · me　jiǎn　dān · de.

The truth is not as simple as that.

153